Information Literacy
Navigating & Evaluating Today's Media

Second Edition

Author

Sara Armstrong, Ph.D.

SHELL EDUCATION

Information Literacy:
Navigating & Evaluating Today's Media

Editor
Diana Herweck, Psy.D.

Assistant Editor
Leslie Huber, M.A.

Editorial Director
Dona Herweck Rice

Editor-in-Chief
Sharon Coan, M.S.Ed.

Editorial Manager
Gisela Lee, M.A.

Creative Director
Lee Aucoin

Cover Design
Lee Aucoin

Interior Layout Designer
Robin Erickson

Print Production
Juan Chavolla

Publisher
Corinne Burton, M.A.Ed.

Shell Education
5301 Oceanus Drive
Huntington Beach, CA 92649-1030
http://www.shelleducation.com
ISBN 978-1-4258-0554-8

© *2008 Shell Education*

Reprinted 2011

Table of Contents

About This Book 7

Part 1: READY— Information Is Everywhere 9

Chapter 1: Introduction to Information Literacy 11

Activity: Information Sources, Systems,
    and Devices Time Line 14

Activity: Information Literacy Then & Now 17

Chapter 2: Information: Where Does It Come From? 21

Visual Literacy 23

Why Visual Literacy? 24

Activity: Pictures and Words 29

Television 31

Activity: What Do You See? 33

TV-Viewing Data Sheet 35

TV-Viewing Data Sheet Sample 37

Activity: TV Humor 39

TV Humor Activity Sheet 41

TV Humor Activity Sheet Sample 43

Activity: TV Ads 45

TV Ads Activity Sheet 47

TV Ads Activity Sheet Sample 49

Websites 52

Checklist for an Information Web Page 54

Activity: If It's on the Web, It Must Be True 57

Website Data Sheet 59

Website Data Sheet Sample 61

Activity: Five Criteria 63

Five Criteria Activity Sheet 65

Five Criteria Activity Sheet Sample 66

Part 2: SET— Using Information. 67

Chapter 3: Good Question! 69
Grazing the Net: Raising a Generation of
Free-Range Students 71
Educational Strategies. 75
Bloom's Taxonomy "Revised" Key Words, Model
Questions, & Instructional Strategies. 77
Asking Good Questions 83
Activity: What Is the Question? 85
Question Activity Sheet 89
Activity: What Do They Really Mean?. 91
Assumptions Activity Sheet 93

Chapter 4: Organizing Information 95
Activity: Graphic Organizer Practice 102
Activity: Storyboard 104

Chapter 5: Where Did That Come From? 107
Copyright. 107
Fair Use 109
Creative Commons. 110
The Educator's Guide to Copyright and Fair Use 112
Activity: The Copyright Quiz 115
Activity: Student Copyright Scenarios 119
Copyright Scenarios 121
Citing Sources 123
Activity: Who You Gonna Call? 126
Permission Request Activity Sheet 129
Activity: Citing Sources 131
Citing Sources Activity Sheet—MLA Style 134
Citing Sources Activity Sheet—APA Style 136

Chapter 6: Search Techniques and Strategies 139

Four NETS for Better Searching 139

Search Strategies Activity Sheet 146

Chapter 7: The World of Libraries 147

Using Primary Sources in the Classroom 162

Lesson Suggestions 162

Activity: Word Study 169

Word Card Template and Example 172

Activity: Library Linkup 173

Library Information Sheet 175

Library Information Sheet Sample 176

Part 3: GO!— Harnessing Information 177

Chapter 8: It's a 2.0 World 179

Online Interactions 180

Netiquette. 180

Cyber Safety 181

Cyber Bullying 181

Focus on Writing. 182

Blogs. 182

Wikis 185

Podcasts 187

Other Social-Networking Tools 187

Activity: Web 2.0 Tools. 190

Chapter 9: Developing and Evaluating Multimedia Projects . . 193

Project Design 194

Project Assessment 199

Activity: Developing a Project-Based Learning Project 202

Project-Based Learning Activity Sheet 204

Activity: Creating a Project-Based Learning Rubric 205

Evaluation Rubric Activity Sheet 207

Evaluation Rubric Activity Sheet Sample 208

Part 4: RESOURCES 209
   Print Material. 209
   Websites by Chapter 212
   Specialized Search Engines and Directories 223
   Directories Especially for Educators 223
   Search Engines and Databases Not Just for Educators 224
   The Copyright Quiz Answers. 227
   Copyright and Fair Use Guidelines for Teachers 230
   Acknowledgements. 232

About This Book

We live in a world of information. Learning how to handle it all has become a lifelong task. Teachers and students benefit from being able to locate, evaluate, and use information. To that purpose, this book was created, with explanations, activities, and activity sheets to support the harnessing and understanding of information.

The book is divided into four sections:

Part 1: READY—Information Is Everywhere: This section gets us into the conversation. What is information? What are the information sources we encounter every day? How can we make sense of all we see and hear?

Chapter 1: Introduction to Information Literacy
Chapter 2: Information: Where Does It Come From?

Part 2: SET—Using Information: This section provides opportunities to practice using information wisely.

Chapter 3: Good Question!
Chapter 4: Organizing Information
Chapter 5: Where Did That Come From?
Chapter 6: Search Techniques and Strategies
Chapter 7: The World of Libraries

Part 3: GO!—Harnessing Information: This section provides guidelines for moving from data to information to knowledge— producing information.

Chapter 8: It's a 2.0 World
Chapter 9: Developing and Evaluating Multimedia Projects

The culminating activity in chapter 9 challenges students to bring together everything they have learned in this book as they develop, complete, and present a project-based learning project.

Part 4: RESOURCES: This section concludes the book, along with my challenge to you to decide on a proactive step you will take, whether it's trying an activity with your students, checking out an interesting website, or looking into one of the books in the resources section.

It is my hope that the variety of articles, ideas, resources, and activities in this book will provide information and fresh thinking about what it means to be fully functioning intellectually in this digital age.

Part 1:
READY—

Information Is Everywhere

Chapter 1

Introduction to Information Literacy

There is no question that we are overwhelmed with information, or, more accurately, overwhelmed with faceless data flooding us from every quarter.

—David Thornburg (Starsong 2006)

From the moment we wake up each day until the moment we go to sleep at night, we are bombarded with words, pictures, sounds, and smells, all presented in a dizzying array of media. Our job—an increasingly difficult one—is to make sense of what we encounter. As educators, our main focus is on students: helping them become confident, critical thinkers and users of information from all the sources they encounter.

The hope of education is that data becomes information, which becomes knowledge, which, if we are lucky, leads to understanding (or, some say, wisdom). The process of thinking, assessing, acting upon, assimilating, and discarding unusable data lasts forever and can be improved upon continuously. I believe that good teachers go into the field of education and stay there because they are as intrigued and caught up in learning every day as are their best students. This becomes all the more important as the world shrinks; we get to know more and more of our neighbors, and available information increases exponentially.

Two organizations—the Metiri Group and the Partnership for 21st Century Skills—have done research about what employers expect from students who hope to join their workforce. What both groups have uncovered is the idea that while reading, writing, and arithmetic are extremely important, there are other skill sets that schools generally do not cover that are vital as well.

The Metiri Group (**http://www.metiri.com**) divides the skills into four categories: Digital-Age Literacies, Inventive Thinking, Effective Communication, and High Productivity. (See the Metiri Group's matrix at **http://www.metiri.com/features.html**.)

Both groups agree that students need more practice with collaborating, thinking critically, engaging with a variety of sources, working with technology tools, and creating high-quality work. Project-based learning, which is the hoped-for culmination of all the processes and skills laid out in this book, provides excellent opportunities for building and increasing twenty-first-century skills.

The International Society for Technology in Education (ISTE) recently updated its Educational Technology Standards for Students. It is gratifying to note that these standards are much less tool-based than in the past and also support the twenty-first-century skill ideas described above. The six categories follow:

- Creativity & Innovation
- Communication & Collaboration
- Research & Information Fluency
- Critical Thinking, Problem Solving, & Decision Making
- Digital Citizenship
- Technology Operations & Concepts

Take a look at the ISTE website for more information and detailed explanations **(http://www.iste.org/Content/NavigationMenu/ NETS/For_Students/NETS_S.htm)**.

The idea that students need tools to evaluate what they see and hear becomes more compelling with recent findings from brain-based research. Since preexisting knowledge—that is, what students come to school knowing or thinking they know—is such a powerful force, it is incumbent upon teachers to assess student thinking.

A number of effective teaching and learning strategies can be supported by the information and activities in this book. For example, Gardner's theory of the multiple intelligences honors the many ways we take in and process information—the ways we learn best. Gardner suggests there are at least eight intelligences: linguistic (i.e., those who like words and language), logical mathematical (i.e., those who enjoy numbers and logic), spatial (i.e., those who are conscious of where they are in space), musical (i.e., those who play instruments and sing, as well as those who appreciate music), bodily kinesthetic (i.e., those who need to move in order to learn and who love physical activity), naturalist (i.e., those who enjoy nature and work well with patterns), intrapersonal (i.e., those who learn first on their own), and interpersonal (i.e., those who learn first with others). The multiple intelligences of learners can be honored by engaging students in work that allows them to move, draw, talk about their learning, and explore ideas, patterns, and a variety of forms of expression.

Project-based learning suggests that teachers provide opportunities for students to develop cross-curricular activities that challenge their thinking and deepen their understanding of a problem or task. There are ideas throughout this book that could be executed as meaningful projects. Chapter 9 brings it all together with a focus on building and evaluating project-based learning projects.

Activity: Information Sources, Systems, and Devices Time Line

Introduction:

Throughout time, the need to gather and evaluate information has been a survival skill. In this activity, students will create a time line of important milestones in history having to do with the development of information sources, systems, and devices. Starting, perhaps, with the development of spoken languages, students will explore other communication processes (e.g., smoke signals, written language, books and newspapers, radio, television, the Internet) and work together to develop a time line of these developments. You may want to focus the information sources, systems, and devices that students will research, because trying to cover everything from 35,000 B.C. to the present is an overwhelming task. However, examining the history of communication and the advances that have been made is a fascinating study.

Objectives:

- Students will research milestones in communication throughout time.
- Students will reflect on the myriad information sources available today.

Materials:

- resources, including books, textbooks, websites; paper and pencil; large-screen computer hookup with mind-mapping software such as *Inspiration*®; large board with markers or easel paper and markers

Procedure:

1. Introduce the idea of communication—one to one and one to many—and how people throughout time have coped with the need to know important information.

2. Brainstorm with students as many communication devices as possible. Suggest that students group the devices in various ways, such as written, visual, or audio, or by their earliest introduction. Jot down these ideas.

3. Show or invite students to explore a variety of sources that examine communication time lines or specific devices, such as their textbooks or these references:

- About.com: Inventors: The History of Communication

  http://inventors.about.com/library/inventors/bl_history_of_communication.htm

- Wikipedia: History of Communication

  http://en.wikipedia.org/wiki/History_of_communication

- Nathan: Projects: A History of Communications 35,000 B.C.–1998 A.D.

  (Nathan Sherdoff is an entrepreneur, researcher, author, and speaker who focuses on experiential learning, business, and new technologies.)

  http://www.nathan.com/projects/current/comtimeline.html

- A World of Communication, ThinkQuest, 1999

  http://library.thinkquest.org/26890/

- Federal Communications Commission: History of Communication

  http://www.fcc.gov/omd/history/

- NASA History Division: Communications Satellites Short History

  http://www.hq.nasa.gov/office/pao/History/satcomhistory.html

- *A History of Mass Communication: Six Information Revolutions* by Irving Fang, Focal Press, 1997.

4. Suggest that students work in small groups and focus their research on different time periods related to your social studies standards.

5. Have the groups work collaboratively to share what they have learned and add to the time line. (You can create a physical time line to post on the classroom wall, or you can develop a time line online.)

6. Suggest that students draw illustrations of the information sources they identify, and post them on the time line.

7. The time line can be modified throughout the year as more areas of study are undertaken.

8. At a later date, ask students to consider communication needs of the future. Ask students to develop a short presentation of their ideas.

Reflection:

By considering all the ways we currently share and take in information and the ways we may need to do so in the future, students develop an awareness of information sources and needs. As they explore different kinds of communication over time, the idea of education and the importance of shared ideas can be examined.

Activity: Information Literacy Then & Now

Introduction:

The purpose of this activity is for students to begin to examine the amount of information they encounter every day, as compared to information their parents or other adults encountered as schoolchildren.

Objectives:

- Students will interview adults about information sources of the past.

- Students will reflect on information sources available today.

- Students will make comparisons and reflect on today's possibility for "information overload."

Materials:

- paper and pencil, computer, video camera or other means of recording interview information

Procedure:

1. Review the time line created in the previous activity. Have the class brainstorm a list of information sources available today (e.g., books, TV news, websites, magazines, video conferences, cell phone pictures).

2. Have students discuss the kinds of information sources available to their parents and grandparents when they were students of the same age.

3. Have students work in pairs to develop questions they will ask parents and grandparents about information sources available to them when they were in elementary or secondary school. They should include questions about how their parents and grandparents evaluated the information they received, as well as questions that

will elicit opinions about sources available today, and how we know whether we can trust the information we encounter.

4. Using the questions developed, have students interview their parents and grandparents. Working again in pairs, ask students to compile their information and develop a short presentation about information sources then and now, the importance of access to information, and the skills needed then versus the skills needed now for assessing available information.

5. Bonus question for the class to discuss: What information sources and/or communication processes will be developed in the future, and how should they be evaluated for credibility?

Reflection:

When students engage in intergenerational conversations, their understanding of aspects of their own lives grows deeper. Inviting parents, grandparents, and community members to school so that students can demonstrate their understanding creates a powerful learning community that extends beyond school walls.

Activity: Information Literacy Then & Now *(cont.)*

Sample Interview Questions:

1. What communication devices do you rely on most (e.g., telephone, newspaper, TV, cell phone, Internet)?

2. How old were you when you watched your first television show?

3. What were your favorite TV shows when you were my age?

4. Do you remember how much stamps cost when you were my age?

5. What do you think have been the most important developments in communication in your lifetime? Why?

6. How do you know whether you can believe what you see on TV or read in the newspaper today? Is this different from when you were my age?

7. What advice do you have for kids today in terms of how they should evaluate what they see on TV or the Internet or read in a newspaper?

8. Do you think the value of encyclopedias has changed over time?

9. Is there any modern communication device you think we should eliminate? Why?

10. Do you have any ideas for a new invention that would aid communication?

Chapter 2

Information:
Where Does It Come From?

Phillip Seymour, in his article "Media Literacy: Seeing, Believing, and Understanding the Power of Images," explains the importance of working with students to increase media literacy. He says,

> *Media saturates our culture, affects the brain development of our students, and enters every fabric of our conscious and unconscious lives. Most schools are not teaching the thinking skills needed to analyze and critically evaluate what is seen, heard, and experienced in the media. This leaves students vulnerable to mass media's marketing of ideas, information, and products. Additionally, the Internet offers a vast, unregulated universe of information that requires critical and evaluative analysis.*

(From "Visual Learning: The Power of Images," Polaroid Education Program, June 2003; available as a PDF. Go to **http://www.polaroid. com**, select your country, then enter "Visual Learning Newsletter" in the Search box. Click on "Seeing Growing Learning," then on "VLF Newsletter: Media Literacy" for Seymour's full article.)

Most of us have five senses: sight, smell, taste, hearing, and touch. These senses define our interactions with the world, inspire our thoughts, and make our experiences meaningful. Currently, two senses are most often affected by the kinds of information discussed in this book: sight and hearing. At school, we usually talk about three ways in which information is presented: through images, through written words, and through verbal instructions or conversations.

In his book *Information Anxiety 2* (QUE 2001), Richard Saul Wurman reminds us that a man of the seventeenth century encountered less information in his lifetime than we can read in a weekday issue of *The New York Times* today. Others remind us that it takes 18 months—or less—for the amount of information in the world to double. Along with the amount of information, the sources from which information originates have proliferated. You may want to brainstorm with your students as many sources of information as you can name. Many of them combine text, images, and sound in a variety of ways:

Books	TV	Radio billboards	Recipes
Magazines	Movies	Concerts	Manuals
Newspapers	Video games	Plays	Forms
Journals	CDs, DVDs	Records	Maps
Pamphlets	VHS tapes	Sheet music	Ads
Stories	Cassette tapes	Pictures	Tests
Email	Websites	Charts, graphs	Paintings

In this chapter, we will be focusing on images, TV, print material, and websites in terms of awareness, understanding, and evaluation of messages. I suggest that similar kinds of evaluation activities be developed for each information source from every medium. In this way, we can help sensitize students to the idea that they should question everything they see and hear, particularly if the intent of the information is to motivate or convince.

We could name a literacy for each of the sources of information listed above; that is, we could define the aspects and criteria for the evaluation of image literacy, TV literacy, print literacy, etc. I believe this is a good idea, if only to focus on the awareness and critical thinking skills we must build in regard to each information source.

For now, let's look at visual literacy (i.e., ways to work with images) and print literacy (i.e., ways to work with text, particularly in books, magazines, journals, and on websites). In the course of mastering these literacies, we will engage in understanding information that comes to us through a combination of media, such as movies, TV, and the Internet.

Visual Literacy

In an article in the *San Francisco Chronicle*, the paper's Arts Culture critic, Steven Winn, wrote about the power of images in text:

> *Kids know it better than the rest of us do: Words and pictures are primally bound.... Kids don't look at pictures as diverting illustrations or supplements to the text. They read pictures avidly, mining them for every bit of information, mood, feeling, mystery and nuance of the world fanning open before them. Every picture tells a thousand stories. From the Cat in the Hat to the Koran, illustrations have the power to illuminate. (San Francisco Chronicle*, Aug. 21, 2003)

Since images are so integral in learning (research states that 80 percent of what we take in and remember is in the form of images), the importance of developing visual literacy is critical.

Lynell Burmark, Ph.D., has been engaged in working with images for quite some time. She has helped teachers and students understand the impact of images in their work, including specialized aspects such as the influence of color.

In the following excerpt from her book *Visual Literacy: Learn to See, See to Learn*, Burmark lays the foundation for thoughtful examination of images in a variety of media, and she encourages us to deepen our understanding so that we can make powerful choices of images when we create our own information sources.

Why Visual Literacy?

By Lynell Burmark, Ph.D.

Now the truth can be told: Students learn more, faster, and retain information better with image-rich instruction. No one doubts the need for print literacy: reading and writing words. I would advocate that visual literacy—reading and writing images—is an even more basic skill.

Lou Fournier Marzeles

My colleague Lou Fournier Marzeles sent me this picture that he took at the Palatki Indian ruins just north of Sedona, Arizona. The small hand was imprinted on the stone walls around 5000 B.C. It makes me think of the walls covered with graffiti in many of our modern cities. Mankind wants to communicate, to say: "Look! I was here." This reaching out tends to be, as it was 5,000 years ago, in the form of the most basic visual (rather than textual) communications.

Our Visual World

Today, we clearly live in a visual world. Our news comes through visual media: illustrated magazines and newspapers, movies and television, and visually engaging sites with streaming video from the Internet. Thanks to ubiquitous televisions, a world of events unfolds in our living rooms. Who can ever forget the planes crashing into the twin towers of the World Trade Center on September 11, 2001?

Our youth have grown up with television. The average teen has watched about 22,000 hours by the time he or she graduates from high school. (Compare this to the 12,500 hours spent sitting in classrooms!)

And our children are encountering the very visual medium of computers at an earlier and earlier age.

Lynell Burmark

Brain Bandwidth

As human beings, our brains are wired for images. According to research from 3M Corporation, we process visuals 60,000 times faster than text. This is because we take in all the data from an image simultaneously, while we process text in a sequential fashion.

I could tell you about my wonderful former boss and the love he feels for his first granddaughter. Or I could show you the photo:

Susan Elshire

Which is faster? Which is more memorable?

From Images to Words

There is a natural progression in the way we process information: first the image, then the words. We run into trouble in school when we try to reverse that order, when teachers use words and assume every student sees the same image.

For example, what if I, as the teacher, say the word *tree*? If you live in Olean, New York, you would probably see a sugar maple tree. From West Palm Beach, Florida? A row of palm trees. Or if you grew up in Tacoma, Washington, the way I did, you might see a cedar, fir, or some other evergreen tree. Is one of these trees any more "correct" than the others? (Is there always just one right answer?)

A letter was recently circulating the Internet describing a young boy's reaction to this beautiful sunset:

Commander John Bortniak, NOAA Corps (retired)
National Oceanic and Atmospheric Administration
Department of Commerce

"Dear God, I didn't think purple and orange went together until I saw the sunset you created on Tuesday. That was cool."

—Eugene

"I didn't think...until I saw." The image always precedes the thought. Einstein imagined riding on a beam of light and then did the math to back up his theory of relativity. First the image, then the thought.

Lou Fournier Marzeles put it most succinctly when he summarized my research in this area into one catchy phrase: "What You Get Is What You See," or WYGIWYS. (This is, of course, a play on the term WYSIWYG, which described the breakthrough in the early '80s when we first were able to see on the computer screen what we were going to get on the printer.)

Multimedia, Multiple Streams

But is all that multimedia really necessary? Are videos anything more than a way to babysit students on a Friday afternoon? Aren't all these images more distracting than helpful? More decoration or entertainment than substance?

Quite the contrary. Research is showing that with multiple streams of information coming in, students have greater focus. They learn more, faster, and remember the information longer. As one young man expressed it, the traditional chalk-and-talk classrooms are like going down the freeway at 30 miles per hour. You have plenty of time to get distracted and bored. The multiple streams, multimedia approach is like traveling at 80 miles an hour. You have to concentrate, or you will crash and burn.

So, really, what we are talking about is transforming classrooms from boring places where students ask, "Why do I have to learn this?" to engaging places where students ask, "Why do I have to leave now?"

We are advocating breaking down the walls and opening classrooms to the world of experiences that lies beyond—traveling from Alaska …to Hawaii…to outer space…and everywhere in between. We can talk until the cows come home, but unless our words, concepts, and ideas are hooked onto an image, they will go in one ear, sail through the brain, and go out the other ear. Words are processed by our short-term memory, where we can only retain about seven bits of information (plus or minus two). This is why, by the way, we have seven-digit phone numbers. Images, on the other hand, go directly into our long-term memory, where they are indelibly etched. Images we share with students will be with them forever (not just for the test).

As parents and educators, we have the responsibility and the opportunity to expand students' data banks of images, to select images of beauty and truth, of love and devotion, of inspiration and hope for the future.

That is the mission of visual literacy.

Lynell Burmark, Ph.D., is an award-winning educator, author, and speaker whose specialties include strategies for successful presentations, resources for early literacy, multimedia for multiple intelligences, creativity and connectivity, the power of more visual teaching and learning, career-life-mission planning, event marketing and management, and "enlightening up" for stress-free living. She can be reached at **Lynell@ educatebetter.org**.

Activity: Pictures and Words

Introduction:

Companies design logos and catch phrases to market their products. In this activity, students will work in pairs to collect 10 examples of a company logo and catch phrase (e.g., Nike's swoosh and "Just Do It."). Students will write an appraisal of how well the logo and catch phrase (i.e., visual and verbal representation of an idea) go together and how well they work as a marketing tool for the company.

Objectives:

- Students will become aware of a marketing technique: company identity through logo and catch phrase.

- Students will reflect on these marketing tools and how successful they are.

Materials:

- magazines, Internet access, three-by-five-inch index cards, scissors, glue, paper and pencils

Procedure:

1. Lead a discussion with your class about company logos and catch phrases. Have students suggest a few examples.

2. Have students work in pairs to find examples of 10 company logos and their catch phrases. They might use magazines, from which they can cut out the logos and words, or they might go online and copy logos and words. They might also collect examples outside of school—from billboards, TV, etc.

3. Have students make two sets of cards, one with logos on each card, the other with the catch phrases.

4. Have pairs of students exchange their cards and match logos to catch phrases.

5. Students will then collaborate on a short paper expressing their opinions on the effectiveness of the logos and catch phrases in selling a product.

6. Conclude with a class discussion about logos and catch phrases as marketing tools.

7. Extension: Have students develop a logo and catch phrase for a company they would start, with a written rationale for their choices.

Reflection:

Students' abilities to express thoughtful viewpoints during the discussion will confirm their understanding of the role of logos and catch phrases as marketing tools. A discussion of the power of advertising could take place, in which students reflect on the use of images and words in combination to convince customers of the worth of a product.

Television

We see still and moving pictures in many places. One of the most influential sources of images is television—probably because it's so widespread and many of us spend a considerable amount of time watching it on a daily basis.

In his book *The Smart Parent's Guide to Kids' TV*, Dr. Milton Chen suggests that the most important aspect of television is the content. Any of the sources listed on page 22 has the potential to present quality information. However, the opposite is also true. To help students become thoughtful consumers (and future producers) of information, they must be given the tools with which to analyze the messages they are receiving from the most ubiquitous source of information.

Chen puts forth the idea that other media, including newspapers, magazines, books, and especially the Internet, often contain content that is questionable or bad, but we do not seem to complain about these media in the same way we criticize TV. He asks, "Why the difference? I believe it has to do with the fact that newspapers, radio, and computers, for the most part, belong to adults.... Because TV is such an easy target, it's an easy scapegoat for all that is wrong with society. Television has single-handedly been blamed for increasing crime, reducing levels of education, destroying our values, ruining our workforce, and making us fat" (pages 32–33).

To remedy this situation, a number of organizations have created educational materials for the purpose of putting media into perspective. For example, the National Television Academy has developed a curriculum guide for high school teachers titled, "'If It Bleeds, It Leads' and Other Lessons on Broadcast Journalism," that engages students in a number of exercises and ethical dilemmas that real-life broadcast people encounter. The curriculum guide is available at no charge online (**http://www.nationalstudent. tv/teachersmain.asp**). According to Julie Lucas, who chairs the Education Program for the National Television Academy, the goal is "to foster the next generation of TV journalists and to create a more educated and demanding audience that understands the need for television excellence." Lucas says, "I see the dumbing down of TV content, and audiences that fail to demand the best from programmers, who are responding in kind. So we created lessons that use real-life situations, and we put students right in the thick of it so they can experience what real-life journalists go through, and they could make their own choices about how to resolve the same situations they are seeing on TV."

Topics addressed in the downloadable PDF curriculum guide include how much information to provide, hidden cameras, freedom of expression in today's world, the public's right to know versus the right to privacy, bias in network broadcasts, intellectual property and copyright, and plagiarism.

The National Television Academy—which governs the Emmys—also sponsors a contest for students. Each year, high school students are invited to submit "examples of their finest work in television broadcast, cablecast, and Webcast production." For more information, visit their website (**http://www.nationalstudent.tv/ information.asp**).

Activity: What Do You See?

Introduction:

Even though television has been widely available for a relatively short time, it is highly controversial—whether we look at studies of how much time children spend watching it, or how what children see on TV influences their thoughts and behavior. In this activity, students will become critics as they examine one of their favorite shows. They will focus on point of view and include their own ideas about how the show could have been filmed.

Objectives:

- Students will describe point of view.

- Students will start to think objectively about a TV show.

- Students will begin to identify bias.

- Students will begin to think critically about what they are seeing.

Materials:

- notepaper, pens or pencils, copy of the TV-Viewing Data Sheet (pages 35–36) for each student

Procedure:

1. Lead a class discussion on TV: What do students think about what they see on TV? Do they believe what they see? Why or why not? Include the idea that different shows sometimes present opposite views (e.g., on life, on a particular idea, etc.). Explain that their homework will be to take on the role of a TV critic while watching their favorite shows.

2. Acquaint students with what is meant by *point of view*. (Definitions include "the stance or opinion expressed by someone, or a way of behaving.")

3. Go over the TV-Viewing Data Sheet, and ask students what show they will watch.

4. Encourage students to tape their shows and watch them more than once before they fill out the data sheet.

5. After students have watched their shows and completed the data sheets, lead a discussion about what they learned.

Reflection:

Since TV is such an important part of most students' lives, this activity could be assigned several times by having students follow a different character in their favorite shows, examine different shows, look at the same show over time, etc. Perhaps students could talk with younger peers about their views on particular shows. We want to encourage the thoughtful use of TV and help students realize they always have a choice whether to watch it.

TV-Viewing Data Sheet

Name: _____ Date: _____

Title and date of the show: _____

Select one of the characters and describe what he or she does during the show.

_____

_____

_____

Describe the main event that happens during the show. What is the main point of the show?

_____

_____

_____

Pick one of the other characters and describe what he or she does.

_____

_____

_____

How would you describe the point of view of the first character you chose?

_____

_____

_____

_____

How would you describe the point of view of the other character you chose?

_____

_____

_____

_____

How would an alternate point of view have changed what happens in the show?

_____

_____

_____

Would an alternate point of view have been more meaningful or interesting?

_____

_____

_____

_____

If you had directed the show, what would you have done differently?

_____

_____

_____

_____

_____

TV-Viewing Data Sheet Sample

Name: <u>Sara Armstrong</u>   Date: <u>01/04/07</u>

Title and date of the show: <u>*Ugly Betty* 1/3/07</u>

Select one of the characters and describe what he or she does during the show.

<u>Betty is taking a writing class and has to read a piece she wrote, knowing the instructor is very critical and sarcastic.</u>

Describe the main thing that happens during the show. What is the main point of the show?

<u>The main thing that happens is that Betty reads a story that she didn't write and claims she did as she reads it to the writing class. She is praised for the story, and her instructor contacts a journal to publish it. Then, the real author shows up.</u>

Pick one of the other characters and describe what he or she does.

<u>Daniel, Betty's boss, steps in and ameliorates the situation by paying off the real author. He feels that he has some responsibility because he gave Betty the other person's story by mistake in the first place.</u>

How would you describe the point of view of the first character you chose?

<u>Betty is usually an honest, responsible woman who tries to do the right thing.</u>

How would you describe the point of view of the other character you chose?

<u>Daniel feels that he is not as good at a lot of things as others he cares about: his sister, his father, etc.</u>

How would an alternate point of view have changed what happened in the show?

If Betty had not been confronted by the real author, she might not have told the truth. But she probably would have, because that's who she is.

Would an alternate point of view have been more meaningful or interesting?

No, I think having Betty make a mistake and then confess was very powerful.

If you had directed the show, what would you have done differently?

I would have done what the director did: have Betty become involved in an ethical dilemma and then make it right, with some help, if necessary.

Activity: TV Humor

Introduction:

Humor is an interesting topic. People find different things funny. In this activity, students will do a short survey of how both TV ads and TV shows use humor, and then reflect on why and how it worked.

Objectives:

- Students will explore different kinds of humor presented on TV.

- Students will watch TV shows and TV commercials and categorize the kinds of humor they encounter.

- Students will discuss their findings.

Materials:

- chart paper, copy of the TV Humor Activity Sheet (pages 41–42) for each student

Procedure:

1. Lead a discussion with students on different kinds of humor or the many ways people use humor (e.g., making fun of a person's actions, telling a joke, acting silly). Brainstorm ideas on the board or on a piece of chart paper that can be hung on the wall during the activity.

2. Explain that students will pick a situation comedy or other television show based on humor to view. Students will fill out the TV Humor Activity Sheet based on what they see.

3. Ask students to describe a humorous incident in the show or an overall impression of the humor used during the show.

4. Ask students to tally the number of commercials they saw during the time they were watching the show. Commercials include

everything that is not part of the show, such as ads for products, public service announcements, trailers for upcoming movies or shows, teasers for new shows coming on later, etc.

5. Have students also describe the type of humor used in several select commercials.

6. Ask students to write brief reflections after they have finished watching their shows.

7. Have students discuss their findings. Did they feel that humor was used effectively? Did it make them want to watch the show again or buy the product? Did the use of humor make them more interested in the show or products than they would have been if humor were not used? What are other emotions that they observed advertisers using in order to try to influence people to buy their products (e.g., fear, embarrassment)?

Reflection:

Humor can be used in many ways. Humor can entertain and amuse, put people down, attempt to influence others, or some combination of all of these. The intent of this activity is to call students' attention to the different ways humor is used on TV and to have them reflect on the effectiveness of its use, as well as the possibility for embarrassment, humiliation, or offense if the situation were real.

TV Humor Activity Sheet

Name: _____ Date: _____

Title and date of TV show: _____

Describe one particular incident of humor in the show or give an overview of the type of humor the show used.

_____

_____

_____

Commercials:

1. Company/product:_____

   Describe the humor used:_____

   _____

   _____

2. Company/product:_____

   Describe the humor used:_____

   _____

   _____

3. Company/product:_____

   Describe the humor used:_____

   _____

   _____

4. Company/product:_____

   Describe the humor used:_____

   _____

   _____

TV Humor Activity Sheet Sample

Name: _Sara Armstrong_____ Date: __01/01/08___

Title and date of TV show: _Just for Laughs   1/1/08___

Describe one particular incident of humor in the show or give an overview of the type of humor the show used.

This show is a "candid camera" show where silly or embarrassing things are used to fool bystanders until the filmers point out the camera. Everyone who sees the camera laughs and is a good sport. I wonder if there were other people who didn't find what happened to them so funny. There were silly things like smashing pies into people's faces as they bent to smell them or four people jumping out of a car and picking up a man who had just crossed a street and carrying him back to the other side—several times. There were also two "policemen" who were directing traffic at a roundabout and telling drivers to go in exactly the opposite direction. And there were two "older people" with walkers who would walk in front of traffic and stop. Drivers finally got out of their cars to help them cross the street, but by the time the drivers got back in their cars, the people were blocking their way again.

Commercials:

1. Company/product: _Dance Wars_____

    Describe the humor used: _The two people who will be teaching competing groups of people to sing and dance pretended to be mad at each other, promising to beat the other, etc._

2. Company/product: _Domino's Pizza_____

    Describe the humor used: _Two guys waiting for pizza pretended that the time it took for the pizza to arrive—30 minutes— passed quickly. There were flashbacks to them playing games, jumping around, etc._

3. Company/product: <u>Verizon Wireless</u>

Describe the humor used: <u>Cute—the Verizon guy was taken into a car and told to breathe deeply as if he were going into labor. He said, "Can you hear me now?" as they went into a tunnel. The commercial then switches to an actual pregnant woman trying to call her husband as she heads to the hospital.</u>

4. Company/product: <u>H&R Block</u>

Describe the humor used: <u>Two men in lederhosen were talking about taking deductions on their taxes for their clothing. One told the other all the deductions he'd been able to take; the other agreed that he should contact H&R Block. The humor was in their clothing and all the varieties of it that were mentioned.</u>

Activity: TV Ads

Introduction:

There are a great number of ads on television. In fact, it often seems that we watch more ads than actual TV programming in a given time slot. In this activity, students will identify different kinds of ads, rank their effectiveness, create a graph of types of ads, and reflect on why they think certain ads worked while others did not.

Objectives:

- Students will become aware of the number and kinds of ads on TV.

- Students will form opinions on the effectiveness of ads.

Materials:

- copy of TV Ads Activity Sheet (pages 47–48) for each student, paper and pencils

Procedure:

Note: This activity can be altered for younger children. They might simply list the ads and then bring the list into class to talk about. Or, students could draw pictures of their favorite ads and explain why they were their favorites. And, you can suggest variations on the tallying and presentation of the data based on how comfortable your students are with decimals, fractions, and graphs.

1. Point out that a large proportion of a TV show's time slot is often spent in commercials. Explain that the class will be doing some research into the number and kinds of ads on TV and begin to look at why they are effective.

2. Review the TV Ads Activity Sheet and ask students to fill it out over the course of a half-hour of watching TV. They will probably want to take notes before filling in the activity sheet, such as

keeping a list of the kinds of ads during each commercial break.

3. Review how to make either a pie chart or bar graph, which students will use to convey what they learned about the kinds of commercials they saw. Remind students how to convert fractions into percentages, if appropriate.

4. After students have had a chance to fill out their activity sheets, lead a discussion about what was learned. For example, what percentage of commercials during a half hour of evening TV was devoted to particular ads? What information was conveyed?

Reflection:

Because of the pervasiveness of TV ads, this activity might be useful to call attention to the use of advertising to sell particular products. In an extension activity, you might ask students to pick a particular category of products—such as cars, breakfast cereal, or cosmetics—and watch for ads in this category over time, making notes about the effectiveness of the material. A culminating activity might include having students develop public service announcements or ads for a cause they support or a product they want to develop.

TV Ads Activity Sheet

Name: _____ Date: _____

Time slot (day and time):_____

Tally of number of ads: _____

List the companies in the ads (add more numbers if needed):

1. _____

2. _____

3. _____

4. _____

5. _____

6. _____

7. _____

8. _____

9. _____

10. _____

11. _____

12. _____

13. _____

14. _____

15. _____

16. _____

17. _____

18. _____

19. _____

20. _____

Categorize the ads (e.g., financial, TV shows, cars, food, etc.).

1. _____

2. _____

3. _____

4. _____

5. _____

Determine the fractions and percentages for each ad category.

1. _____

2. _____

3. _____

4. _____

5. _____

On a separate page, make a pie chart or bar graph of your findings and label it.

Which ad did you think was the most effective? Why?

_____

_____

_____

_____

_____

TV Ads Activity Sheet Sample

Name: Sara Armstrong   Date: 01/01/08

Time slot (day and time): Tuesday, 8:30–9 P.M.

Tally of number of ads: 21

List the companies in the ads (add more numbers if needed):

1. Bank of America

2. DTV—digital TV

3. TV show: *ABC 7 News*

4. Disneyland

5. Chantix tablets—quit smoking

6. H&R Block—tax preparation

7. Slim-Fast

8. Verizon Wireless

9. TV show: *Dance Wars*

10. TV show: *ABC 7 News*

11. Dodge cars

12. Bank of America Visa

13. TV show: *Oprah*

14. Crest mouthwash

15. Vaseline for dry skin

16. Domino's pizza

17. Quaker oatmeal

TV Ads Activity Sheet Sample *(cont.)*

18. Jell-O

19. TV show—*According to Jim* (coming next)

20. TV shows—*Supernanny* and *Wife Swap*

21. TV show—*ABC 7 News*

Categorize the ads (e.g., financial, TV shows, cars, food, etc.).

1. Financial: 3 (Nos. 1, 6, 12)

2. Health/Food/Medicine: 7 (Nos. 5, 7, 14, 15, 16, 17, 18)

3. TV shows: 7 (Nos. 3, 9, 10, 13, 19, 20, 21)

4. Cars: 1 (No. 11)

5. Services: 2 (Nos. 2, 8)

6. Travel: 1 (No. 4)

Determine the fractions and percentages for each ad category:

1. Financial: $\frac{3}{21} = \frac{1}{7} = 14\%$

2. Health/Food/Medicine: $\frac{7}{21} = \frac{1}{3} = 33\%$

3. TV shows: $\frac{7}{21} = \frac{1}{3} = 33\%$

4. Cars: $\frac{1}{21} = 5\%$

5. Services: $\frac{2}{21} = 10\%$

6. Travel: $\frac{1}{21} = 5\%$

TV Ads Activity Sheet Sample *(cont.)*

Make a pie chart or bar graph of your findings and label it.

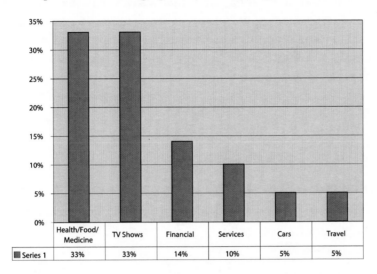

	Health/Food/Medicine	TV Shows	Financial	Services	Cars	Travel
■ Series 1	33%	33%	14%	10%	5%	5%

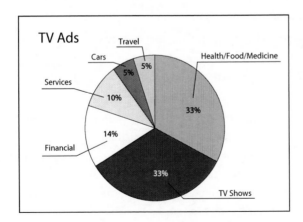

Which ad did you think was the most effective? Why?

<u>I liked the Verizon Wireless ad because it was funny that the guy was pretending to be pregnant as he tested the phone service. It was clever how the commercial then switched to an actual pregnant woman on her way to the hospital to have her baby.</u>

Websites

Jan Alexander and Marsha Ann Tate, reference librarians at Wolfgram Memorial Library at Widener University, have developed a set of criteria that apply to Web pages. These criteria are the same ones the librarians apply to print material they assess for inclusion in the library. Alexander and Tate consider five types of Web pages and suggest five criteria to use to judge whether the sites are trustworthy.

The five types of Web pages include advocacy, business/marketing, news, informational, and personal.

The criteria for judging Web pages include:

1. **Authority**—Who developed the page?
2. **Accuracy**—Can you find additional sources for the information provided on this page?
3. **Objectivity**—Is the page free of bias, or is the bias stated?
4. **Currency**—How recently was the material developed? Has it been updated?
5. **Coverage**—How deeply is the topic addressed? Does the page cite multiple sources?

When looking critically at a Web page, after identifying the purpose of the page and a student's reason for citing it, one or more of the criteria may become more important than weighing all five equally. For example, if I am looking at a personal page, I probably will not expect much objectivity, deep coverage or, perhaps, even accuracy. However, with a page that will be used as research for a paper, I will be concerned about all five criteria. If you are encouraging students to examine primary sources, such as those found at the Library of Congress (**http://www.loc.gov**), you could conduct a discussion with students about the importance of each of the five criteria. Students should at least be able to defend their decisions to use a site after having judged the importance of each criterion in a given context.

The following checklist can be found at **http://www3.widener. edu/Academics/Libraries/Wolfgram_Memorial_Library/Evaluate_ Web_Pages/Checklist_for_an_Information_Web_Page/5720/**. See also **http://www3.widener.edu/Academics/Libraries/Wolfgram_ Memorial_Library/Evaluate_Web_Pages/Original_Web_ Evaluation_Materials/6160/** for links to *PowerPoint* presentations on website evaluation and links to Web pages that include checklists for the other kinds of Web pages. Jan Alexander and Marsha Ann Tate graciously gave permission for the checklist to be reproduced here.

Checklist for an Information Web Page

How to Recognize an Information Web Page

An information Web page is one whose purpose is to present factual information. The URL address frequently ends in .edu or .gov, as many of these pages are sponsored by educational institutions or government agencies (e.g., directories, transportation schedules, calendars of events, statistical data, and other factual information such as reports, presentations of research, or information about a topic).

Questions to Ask About the Web Page

Note: The greater number of questions listed below that can be answered "yes," the more likely it is you can determine that the source is of high information quality.

Criterion #1: AUTHORITY

1. Is it clear who is responsible for the content of the page?

2. Is there a link to a page describing the purpose of the sponsoring organization?

3. Is there a way of verifying the legitimacy of the page's sponsor? That is, is there a phone number or postal address to contact for more information? (Simply providing an email address is not enough.)

4. Is it clear who wrote the material, and are the author's qualifications for writing on this topic clearly stated?

5. If the material is protected by copyright, is the name of the copyright holder given?

Criterion #2: ACCURACY

1. Are the sources for any factual information clearly listed so they can be verified by another source?

2. Is the information free of grammatical, spelling, and typographical errors? (These kinds of errors not only indicate a lack of quality control but can actually produce inaccuracies in information.)

3. Is it clear who is ultimately responsible for the accuracy of the material?

4. If there are charts and/or graphs containing statistical data, are the charts and/or graphs clearly labeled and easy to read?

Criterion #3: OBJECTIVITY

1. Is the information provided as a public service?

2. Is the information free of advertising?

3. If there is any advertising on the page, is it clearly differentiated from the informational content?

Criterion #4: CURRENCY

1. Are there dates on the page to indicate the following?

    a. when the page was written

    b. when the page was first placed on the Web

    c. when the page was last revised

2. Are there any other indications that the material is kept current?

3. If material is presented in graphs and/or charts, is it clearly stated when the data was gathered?

4. If the information is published in different editions, is it clearly labeled which edition the page is from?

Criterion #5: COVERAGE

1. Is there an indication that the page has been completed and is not still under construction?

2. If there is a print equivalent to the Web page, is there a clear indication of whether the entire work is available on the Web?

3. If the material is from a work that is out of copyright (as is often the case with a dictionary or thesaurus), has there been an effort to update the material to make it more current?

Note: This checklist is the original Web version. A revised and expanded version can be found in the authors' book, *Web Wisdom: How to Evaluate and Create Information Quality on the Web*.

Activity: If It's on the Web, It Must Be True

Introduction:

Students often think that everything on the Web must be true. Web pages usually look very professional, and the idea that they are not all created equal is not obvious. In this activity, students will find a Web page of interest to them and then confirm the information on the Web page with two other sources.

Objectives:

- Students will use a data sheet to confirm the veracity of the information.

- Students will identify three sources of information.

- Students will question the wisdom of relying on a single website for information.

Materials:

- access to a computer and the Internet, copies of the Website Data Sheet (pages 59–60) for the students

Procedure:

1. Ask students to identify who can develop and post websites. Ask students how they can determine whether they can trust what they see on the Web.

2. Introduce the Website Data Sheet and tell students they will work in pairs. First, they will each identify a topic and develop a question they will research on the Internet (e.g., Skateboards: Who developed them?).

3. Have students record their topics and questions on the Website Data Sheet and ask permission before proceeding to the computer.

4. Instruct students to go online and find a good website on their topic (i.e., one they feel has good information).

5. Direct students to identify two other sources (e.g., book, article, person) to confirm the information they found on the website.

6. Have students discuss the experience. Were there websites that provided inaccurate information? How difficult was it to find three different sources for the same information? How do you know whom to believe? What other questions arose after doing this research?

Reflection:

When students express the idea that websites are only one source of information and that sometimes they provide incorrect information, the lesson can be considered a success. This activity might be repeated with the initial source as something other than a website (such as a newspaper article or a section of a textbook). Suggest that students find websites on the topic to see if they contain the same information as the initial source. Students may also be shown websites that are designed to misinform or contain erroneous information, such as The Onion (**http://www.theonion.com/content/index**).

Website Data Sheet

Name: _____ Date: _____

Topic: _____

Question: _____

URL: _____

Information to be verified:

_____

_____

_____

What about the website makes you believe the information it provides
is true?

_____

_____

_____

Alternate source: _____

Confirmed: _____

Not confirmed: _____

What about this source makes you believe the information it provides
is true?

_____

_____

_____

Alternate source: _____

Confirmed: _____

Not confirmed: _____

What about this source makes you believe the information it provides
is true?

_____

_____

_____

What questions do you have after doing this research?

_____

_____

_____

_____

_____

Website Data Sheet Sample

Name: <u>Sara Armstrong</u>　　　　　　Date: <u>12/15/07</u>

Topic: <u>Skateboards</u>

Question: <u>Who first developed skateboards?</u>

URL: <u>skateboard.about.com/cs/boardscience/a/brief_history.htm</u>

Information to be verified:

<u>Who invented the skateboard? This site says it can be traced to no one specific individual but that in the 1950s, a number of surfers came up with the idea of surfing sidewalks at the same time.</u>

What about the website makes you believe the information it provides is true?

<u>The author, Steve Cave, is a longtime skateboarder and now writes about skateboarding for a number of magazines and other places. The site is sponsored by the *New York Times*, which has a reputation to uphold, and is dated 2007.</u>

Alternate source: <u>*Encyclopedia Britannica*</u>

Confirmed: <u>pretty close; says it started in the '60s, not '50s</u>

Not confirmed: _____

What about this source makes you believe the information it provides is true?

<u>The *Encyclopedia Britannica* also has a good reputation for accuracy.</u>

Alternate source: <u>Dictionary.com. Online Etymology Dictionary. Douglas Harper, Historian. http://dictionary.reference.com/browse/ skateboard (accessed: December 31, 2007)</u>

Confirmed: <u>This site says skateboards started around 1963 in Southern California. The word came into the dictionary in 1964.</u>

Not confirmed: _____

What about this source makes you believe the information it provides is true?

It is another reference tool that has been ostensibly put together by people with no bias or agenda.

What questions do you have after doing this research?

I wonder if I should still believe the first source that says skateboarding started earlier than the other two. I want to believe it because the author is a real person who has been a skateboarder, but I wonder if the skateboard was actually developed later because the other two sources say the '60s rather than the '50s.

Activity: Five Criteria

Introduction:

The five criteria identified by Alexander and Tate can be applied to many media. In this activity, students will look at the five criteria and apply them to a website. The purpose of this activity is twofold: to help students become aware of how they can judge the usefulness of a website, and to inform students of criteria that are important to keep in mind as they create their own websites.

Objectives:

- Students will become familiar with the five criteria for website evaluation.

- Students will apply the five criteria to a website.

- Students will reflect on how these criteria might be met in their own websites.

Materials:

- board or chart paper, colored dots (select five colors, one for each of the criteria; you will need sets of five dots for each student for each type of website—or give five colored pens to each student so they can draw their own dots), copies of the Five Criteria Activity Sheet (page 65) for each student, Internet access

Procedure:

1. Introduce the students to the five criteria for website evaluation identified by Jane Alexander and Marsha Ann Tate from Wolfgram Memorial Library at Widener University. These five criteria include:

    a. **Authority**: Who wrote the page? How do you know you can trust his or her work?

b. **Accuracy**: Can the material be verified elsewhere? Does the page contain errors of spelling, grammar, etc.?

c. **Objectivity**: Is there advertising on the page? Why is the page on the Internet? What is its purpose?

d. **Currency**: When was the page posted? When was it last updated?

e. **Coverage**: Has the topic been explored in depth? Are there other references or links that support the information?

2. Ask students about the kinds of websites they encounter, such as personal pages, informational sites, news sites, libraries, art galleries, reference materials, company websites, political sites, etc. Label columns on the board or chart paper with these kinds of sites.

3. Ask students to think about which criteria are most important for each kind of website. Have them use their dots or colored pens to indicate the important criteria for each on the board or chart paper.

4. Acquaint students with the Five Criteria Activity Sheet.

5. Have students visit the Web and select a site to evaluate (or assign them a site you have previewed).

6. Have students fill out the activity sheet, and then lead a discussion on what they discovered.

Reflection:

Students' awareness of the five criteria will influence their review of other websites, including their own. Being aware of the criteria and how a website can be evaluated by using them helps students understand how to judge the credibility of information they encounter, especially on the Web.

Five Criteria Activity Sheet

Name: _____ Date: _____

Title and URL of website: _____

_____

Describe how the website fulfills or fails to fulfill each of the five criteria:

1. Authority: _____

   _____

2. Accuracy: _____

   _____

   _____

3. Objectivity: _____

   _____

   _____

4. Currency: _____

   _____

   _____

5. Coverage: _____

   _____

   _____

For this website, which is the most important criterion and why?

_____

_____

_____

_____

_____

_____

_____

Five Criteria Activity Sheet Sample

Name: _Sara Armstrong_   Date: _12/23/07_

Title and URL of website: _Living on the Brink http://library.thinkquest.org/06aug/02242/_

Describe how the website fulfills or fails to fulfill each of the five criteria:

1. Authority: _Students developed the page as part of a contest. The rules of the contest say they have to cite their sources and not plagiarize. Since this website won first place for its age group, I assume the site is well documented and that the judges checked, too. I see that there are sources cited on each page._

2. Accuracy: _Again, the sources cited on the pages reveal the accuracy of the information; spelling and grammar are very good._

3. Objectivity: _There is no advertising on the website; the site is meant to teach students something. There is a bias in the site: that we need to do something about endangered species. The bias is stated clearly and up front._

4. Currency: _The site was posted as part of a 2007 contest, so it is recent and has not needed to be updated._

5. Coverage: _The topic is covered very well. There are many examples, along with citations, original drawings, and music. There are also links to other sites._

For this website, which is the most important criterion and why?

For this site, I think that accuracy and coverage are the two most important criteria because the information presented needs to be accurate and explored in depth.

Part 2:
SET—
Using Information

#50554—Information Literacy

Chapter 3

Good Question!

Questions—and the search for their answers lie at the heart of meaningful learning. Due to increased access to the overwhelming amount of information available today, we all need tools to help us manage it in order to ensure the quality of our living and learning. Helping students formulate good questions—those that are thoughtful, require research and critical thinking, and deepen our understanding of a topic—may be the most important thing we do as educators. One of the most powerful ways of helping students is by modeling the asking of good questions. It is exciting for us to delve deeply into a topic. Formulating the questions that encourage further exploration is both an art and a skill—for teachers as well as students.

Since information is so readily available—especially on the Internet, which some have called the biggest vanity press in the world—it is particularly important that students question what they find. Practicing the criteria for evaluating websites, as shown in the previous chapter, is a good start. In this chapter, we will look more deeply at the Internet, dubbed the "electronic marketplace." It is open, available, and unmanaged, for the most part, so developing questioning strategies has become more important than ever.

Jamie McKenzie, Ed.D., educator and prolific author, says,

> *How do we sort and sift our way past the charlatans and self-anointed frauds of this new electronic marketplace? How do we protect ourselves from the deceitful? For those who work in schools, how do we raise young people capable of finding their way through this maze?*

Powerful questioning is the answer.

Powerful questioning leads to Information Power—the ability to fashion solutions, decisions and plans that are original, cogent, and effective. (p. 3, *Beyond Technology: Questioning, Research, and the Information Literate School*)

Questions lay the foundation for learning, and when students are embedded in thoughtful projects, they engage in highly meaningful work. The increasing interest in project-based learning over the years demonstrates that well-designed projects provide a good challenge. Planning a good project takes time. Teachers who have conducted successful projects are convinced that what students learn in projects goes far beyond what they learn in traditional classes, because they are challenged to make connections across disciplines, as well as to consider real-world concerns. And the start of a good project is found in the questions students and teachers pose for study.

In the following excerpt, McKenzie discusses the importance of good questions and provides some examples. For a fuller treatment of his views on this topic, see the Questioning Toolkit: **http://questioning.org/Q7/toolkit.HTML**.

Note: This is an excerpt from an article that first appeared in the September 1998 issue of *Phi Delta Kappan.*, copyright 1998, Jamie McKenzie, all rights reserved. Reproduction permission granted by Jamie McKenzie, January 2008. See **http://www.fno.org/text/grazing.html** for the full article.

Grazing the Net: Raising a Generation of Free-Range Students

By Jamie McKenzie, Ed.D.

The Question Is the Answer

To be successful [in helping students learn literacy skills to deal with today's "information abundance"], we must emphasize the development of questioning skills, and we must replace topical research with projects requiring original thought.

Questioning may be the most powerful technology we have ever invented and can give to our students. Questions are the tools required for us to "make up our minds" and develop meaning.

Unless we are connecting with the Internet for mere "edutainment," student questioning must be intense before, during, and after visiting cyberspace.

We must teach students to start their explorations with "essential questions" in mind. They then develop a rich web of related questions that organize and direct the search for insight.

Essential questions spawn inquiries that often extend over a month or a lifetime, questions worth asking, which touch upon basic human issues, investigations that might make a difference in the quality of life, and studies that might cast light in dark corners, illuminating basic truths.

Once they have listed pertinent questions, we must teach students how to conduct a thorough research study. Questioning persists throughout all stages of such an inquiry, as students seek pertinent information … data that will cast light upon (or illuminate) the essential question.

Sample Research Question (Secondary)

"Imagine that you and your partners have been hired as consultants by the states of Washington and Oregon to recommend new policies to stem the decline of the salmon runs during the past decade. Use the Internet, as well as books, newspapers, interviews, and all other appropriate resources, to identify useful practices already tested around the globe, and then determine the applicability of these practices to the particular conditions and needs of the Northwest. How might these strategies be improved? Create a multimedia report for the two governors, sharing specific action recommendations as well as the evidence sustaining your proposals."

Unfortunately, schools have traditionally neglected the development of student questioning skills. According to Hyman (1980), for every 38 teacher questions in a typical classroom, there is only one student question. Schoolhouse research, sadly, has too often fallen into the "go find out about" category. Topical research (e.g., "Go find out about Dolly Madison") requires little more than information gathering.

We must move past projects that are little more than searches for answers to simple questions. We must stop asking for the educational equivalent of fast food. No more trivial pursuit.

Instead of asking students to find out all they can about a particular state or nation, for example, we should be asking them to make a choice.

"Where should your family relocate?"

They compare and contrast several states or cities—sifting, sorting, and weighing the information to gain insight, to make a decision, or to solve a problem.

Sample Research Question (Elementary)

"Imagine that your parents have been given job offers in each of the three following cities: New Orleans, Seattle, and Chicago. Knowing of your access to the Internet, they have asked you to help them decide which city will be the best for the family. Before gathering your information, discuss and identify with them the criteria for selecting a home city. Create a persuasive multimedia presentation showing the strengths and weaknesses of each city on the criteria your family considers important."

Conducting the old topical research with electronic information is a bit like pedaling a tricycle on the interstate. To mix metaphors, classic school research projects (i.e., finding out about a particular state) are too much like shooting at sitting ducks. In an age of information abundance (or glut), they may be quasi-suicidal for teachers. Be ready for hundred-page research papers that have been downloaded, cut and pasted with relatively little reading, thought, or synthesis.

Topical research in this new Information Landscape is the enemy of thought. We are beginning to see a "New Plagiarism," which is simply the old plagiarism abetted by a much more powerful electronic shovel. Stealing other folks' ideas and intellectual property has become much easier. Packaging a paper with a slick appearance has also been simplified.

This decade is the Age of Glib. Volume passes for understanding. Surface is preferred to depth. Even adult thinkers (e.g., reporters, pundits, commentators) indulge in sound bites, mind bytes, eye candy, and mind candy.

If we insist that research focus upon essential questions, we may have an antidote to the New Plagiarism and the Age of Glib. We pose questions that require fresh thought. Our students must make answers, not simply gather them.

McKenzie is an internationally known speaker and writer with a focus on questioning, thinking skills, information literacies, and the smart use of new technologies. McKenzie is also the editor of several online journals: *From Now On—The Educational Technology Journal*; *The Question Mark*, a journal devoted to effective questioning and thinking; and *No Child Left*, a journal attacking the No Child Left Behind legislation. Visit **http://fno.org/JM/subscribe.html** to subscribe to these journals, or you can contact McKenzie at **fromnowon@earthlink.net**.

Educational Strategies

One proven method of engaging students in the process of asking and answering good questions is project-based learning. Most teachers already provide project opportunities for their students, and a number have taken the next step and formalized this type of process much more broadly. The term *project-based learning* can point to a number of different practices, so I would like to define it. In my view, project-based learning refers to a practice whereby students and teachers explore important questions on a variety of topics. Students are engaged in choosing the topic they will research and developing the questions they will answer in the project. The project is often interdisciplinary, students may work with experts (virtually or in reality) to further their studies, and presentations to appropriate audiences play a key role in demonstrating understanding of the topic. Students often work in groups, and products can include reports, videos, websites, constructions, artwork, and other presentations to authentic audiences, such as peers, younger children, community members, experts, and parents.

The Buck Institute for Education is a group dedicated to "improving the practice of teaching and the process of learning." In the institute's recent second edition of its *Project Based Learning Handbook*, educators learn about the history of project-based learning, find many examples of such, and gain solid information about the process of creating and implementing good projects. The institute considers "driving questions" the key to successful projects. Driving questions are those that go deeply into a subject, creating many opportunities for students to research, explore, think, evaluate, synthesize, and discuss. To learn more about the institute or to order the book, visit **http://www.bie.org/index.php**.

Bloom's Taxonomy is familiar to most teachers, and it is considered a tried-and-true way to look at different kinds of learning experiences and determine how much thinking is required on the part of students.

At Indiana University-Purdue University Indianapolis's (IUPUI) Center for Teaching and Learning, the charts on pages 77–81 were developed to update Bloom's Taxonomy based on the work of Lorin Anderson, a student of Bloom. You will see that the key words are now all verbs, and the highest level of thinking is now "Create"—formerly "Synthesis." Students need to engage in all levels of Bloom's Taxonomy with as much emphasis on the higher-order thinking skills as possible. Asking students to formulate good questions moves them to higher-order thinking and allows them to engage in creative, thoughtful work. Indeed, students at River School in Napa characterize good questions as those that have no set answers, require research and thought, and cannot be answered by copying from a book.

Bloom's Taxonomy "Revised" Key Words, Model Questions & Instructional Strategies

Bloom's Taxonomy (1956) has stood the test of time. Recently, Anderson and Krathwohl (2001) have proposed some minor changes, including the renaming and reordering of the taxonomy. The following charts reflect those recommended changes. Note: The first column suggests words to use for commands, and the second and third columns suggest ways in which all the objectives may be taught and questions elicited.

I. REMEMBER (KNOWLEDGE)

(shallow processing: drawing out factual answers, testing recall and recognition)

Verbs for Objectives	Model Questions	Instructional Strategies
choose	Who?	highlighting
define	Where?	rehearsal
describe	Which one?	memorizing
identify	What?	mnemonics
label	How?	
list	Which is the best one?	
locate	Why?	
match	How much?	
memorize	When?	
name	What does it mean?	
omit		
recite		
recognize		
select		
state		

II. UNDERSTAND (COMPREHENSION)

(translating, interpreting, and extrapolating)

Verbs for Objectives	Model Questions	Instructional Strategies
classify defend demonstrate distinguish explain express extend give example illustrate indicate infer interpret interrelate judge match paraphrase represent restate rewrite select show summarize tell translate	State in your own words. Which are facts? What does this mean? Is this the same as … ? Give an example. Select the best definition. Condense this paragraph. What would happen if … ? State in one word. Explain what is happening. What part doesn't fit? Explain what is meant by …. What expectations are there? Read the graph, table. What are they saying? This represents …. What seems to be … ? Is it valid that …? What seems likely? Show in a graph, table. Which statements support … ? What restrictions would you add? Why does this example … ?	key examples emphasize connections elaborate concepts summarize paraphrase students explain students state the rule create visual representations (e.g., concept maps, outlines, flowcharts, organizers, analogies, pro/con grids) metaphors, rubrics, heuristics

III. APPLY

(knowing when to apply; why to apply; and recognizing patterns of transfer to situations that are new, unfamiliar, or have a new slant for students)

Verbs for Objectives	Model Questions	Instructional Strategies
apply choose dramatize explain generalize judge organize paint prepare produce select show sketch solve use	Predict what would happen if .... Choose the best statements that apply. Judge the effects. What would result ... ? Tell what would happen if .... Tell how, when, where, and why. Tell how much change there would be if .... Identify the results of	modeling cognitive apprenticeships "mindful" practice—not just a "routine" practice part and whole sequencing authentic situations "coached" practice case studies simulations algorithms

IV. ANALYZE

(breaking down into parts, forms)

Verbs for Objectives	Model Questions	Instructional Strategies
analyze categorize classify compare differentiate distinguish identify infer point out select subdivide survey	What is the function of ... ? What's fact? Opinion? What assumptions ... ? What statement is relevant? What motive is there? What conclusions can you make? What does the author believe? What does the author assume? Make a distinction. State the point of view of .... What is the premise? What ideas apply? What ideas justify the conclusion? What's the relationship between ... ? The least essential statements are .... What's the main idea? What's the theme? What fallacies, consistencies, and inconsistencies appear? What literary form is used? What persuasive technique is used? Implicit in the statement is	models of thinking challenging assumptions retrospective analysis reflection through journaling debates discussions and other collaborative learning activities decision-making situations

V. EVALUATE

(according to some set of criteria, and state why)

Verbs for Objectives	Model Questions	Instructional Strategies
appraise compare criticize defend judge	What fallacies, consistencies, inconsistencies appear? Which is more important, moral, better, logical, valid, appropriate? Find the errors.	challenging assumptions journaling debates discussions and other collaborative learning activities decision-making situations

VI. CREATE (SYNTHESIS)

(combining elements into a pattern not clearly there before)

Verbs for Objectives	Model Questions	Instructional Strategies
choose combine compose construct create design develop do formulate hypothesize invent make make up organize originate plan produce role-play tell	How would you test … ? Propose an alternative. Solve the following. How else would you … ? State a rule.	modeling challenging assumptions reflection through journaling debates discussions and other collaborative learning activities design decision-making situations

Web References:

- http://www.coun.uvic.ca/learn/program/hndouts/bloom.html
- http://www.fwl.org/edtech/blooms.html
- http://apu.edu/~bmccarty/curricula/mse592/intro/tsld006.htm
- http://152.30.11.86/deer/Houghton/learner/think/bloomsTaxonomy.html
- http://amath.colorado.edu/appm/courses/7400/1996Spr/bloom.html
- http://www.stedwards.edu/cte/bloomtax.htm
- http://quarles.unbc.edu/lsc/bloom.html
- http://www.wested.org/tie/dlrn/blooms.html
- http://www.bena.com/ewinters/bloom.html
- http://weber.u.washington.edu/~krumme/guides/bloom.html

References:

Anderson, L. W. and Krathwohl, D. R. (2001). *A Taxonomy for learning, teaching, and assessing.*

Bloom, B. S. (Ed.). (1956). *Taxonomy of educational objectives: The classification of educational goals by a committee of college and university examiners.* New York: Longmans.

Maynard, John, University of Texas, Austin

Svinicki, Marilla, University of Texas, Austin

Compiled by the IUPUI Center for Teaching and Learning Revised December 2002.

(This material is no longer available at the IUPUI Center for Teaching and Learning site and can be found at **http://www.ctap4.org/infolit/questions.htm.**)

Asking Good Questions

In his thoughtful essay "Inquiry: The Art of Helping Students Ask Good Questions" (2004), David Thornburg, Ph.D., suggests six criteria for determining whether a question is good:

- The answer is unknown.

- The answer is defensible.

- The question leads to deep research.

- The question can apply at any grade level.

- The focus is on understanding.

- The question leads to other questions.

Thornburg explains, "Questions can take many forms. Some reflect surface knowledge. (Who was the 16th president of the United States?) Others call for observations. (What is the temperature of the ore sample?) But questions that fall under the definition of inquiry are different in scope. Rather than asking for simple responses, inquiry addresses deeper issues. Taken literally, inquiry means not just questioning, but questioning into something. This type of questioning is rich because of the depth of the exploration it encourages, and because each good question typically leads to more questions."

dthornburg@aol.com http://www.tcpd.org May 2004. A PDF of this essay can be downloaded at **http://www.ctap4.org/infolit/ questions.htm** at the bottom of the Web page. Be sure to visit the Inquiry Page (**http://inquiry.uiuc.edu/**) for more information about inquiry and links to units developed by teachers based on inquiry.

As we help students become good questioners, it may be useful to pose the idea of a "Question Scale." Questions that are more concrete and fall in lower levels of Bloom's Taxonomy would "weigh" less than those that are more abstract, encompassing, interesting, and found at higher levels of Bloom's Taxonomy within McKenzie's "essential questions," or match the criteria for inquiry that Thornburg has set out.

To start preparing students for developing good questions, the following activities provide some practice.

To be information literate, students must be able to find information efficiently and effectively, evaluate information critically and competently, and use information accurately and creatively.

My best advice? Always be thinking and questioning and paying attention, particularly to who is telling the story.

Activity: What Is the Question?

Introduction:

Good questions are at the heart of good projects. Starting from what students know and moving toward what they want to know, we can help students delve deeply into a topic.

Objectives:

- Students will develop meaningful questions for projects.
- Students will understand levels of questions (see charts pages 86–87).

Materials:

- board, overhead projector, projected computer screen, or chart paper and pens; copies of the Question Activity Sheet (pages 89–90) for each student

Procedures:

1. Engage the class in a brainstorming session in which students identify topics they would like to explore. These topics can be focused on a central theme (e.g., the Civil War) or a subject area (e.g., poetry), or be completely open-ended. As a class, select a topic and have the students help you fill in a K-W-L-H (page 86). The K-W-L-H technique is credited to Donna Ogle in 1986, who created this model to help students focus their thinking while they are reading. The technique can be applied to any subject area and works well when developing the scope of a project for project-based learning. For a more detailed reference, visit the North Central Regional Educational Laboratory's website (**http://www.ncrel.org/sdrs/areas/issues/students/learning/lr1kwlh.htm**).

K: What we *Know*	W: What we *Want* to learn	L: What we *Learned*	H: *How* can we find out more?
1.			
2.			
3.			
4.			
5.			

2. Have students select one of the brainstormed topics they are interested in and work with a partner to develop initial questions (more specifically, what they want to know about the topic). Introduce the Question Scale to the class. The idea behind this scale is to examine the kinds of questions we are interested in answering. These include factual questions, which require little thinking, and other questions that go deeper into understanding a topic. For example, the Question Scale for a project on pets might look something like the chart on page 87. (A Question Scale would be filled out for each pet under consideration; the example on the following page has been filled out for guinea pigs.)

Big Question: What animals make good pets, and why?

Question Scale/Bloom	Topic: Guinea Pigs			
Remember: Yes/No or Who, Where, or How many?	Do guinea pigs live here?	Who has them for sale?	How much do they cost?	What kind of food do they eat?
Understand: Why or How?	Why do guinea pigs make good pets?	How would a guinea pig fit into my life?		
Apply: If … , what then?	If my guinea pig got sick, what would I have to do?	If I did not like taking care of my guinea pig, what would happen?		
Analyze: How does it compare?	How does caring for a guinea pig compare to other pets?			
Evaluate: What if?	What if I were a guinea pig? What would my life be like?			
Create: What else can I think of?	Can guinea pigs be used for any kind of work?	Are there any inventions for guinea pigs?		

3. Have students work in pairs to make sure they have questions on their topic that satisfy every level of the Question Scale.

Reflection:

As part of the learning process for this activity, students can be asked to reflect on what kinds of questions they find most interesting and why, along with how they might apply the K-W-L-H technique and the Question Scale to other topics such as TV ads. You might also ask students what other types of questions they would add to the Question Scale.

Question Activity Sheet

Name: _____ Date: _____

Topic: _____

Fill in the K-W-L-H chart below with everything you can think of on the topic you have chosen.

What I know:	What I want to learn:	What I learned:	How can I find out more?
1.	1.	1.	1.
2.	2.	2.	2.
3.	3.	3.	3.
4.	4.	4.	4.
5.	5.	5.	5.
6.	6.	6.	6.
7.	7.	7.	7.
8.	8.	8.	8.
9.	9.	9.	9.
10.	10.	10.	10.

Fill in the squares with questions from your K-W-L-H chart.

Question Scale/Bloom	Topic		
Yes/No or Who, Where, or How many?			
Why or How?			
If …, what then?			
How does it compare?			
What if?			
What else can I think of?			

Activity: What Do They Really Mean?

Introduction:

Advertisements in magazines and on TV and the Internet contain assumptions—about the buyer/user and about the product being sold. In this activity, students will go beneath the surface and examine the assumptions behind a selection of ads.

Objectives:

- Students will interpret advertising material for hidden assumptions.

- Students will attempt to identify motives for particular types of ads.

Materials:

- variety of ads from print, TV, and the Internet; copies of the Assumptions Activity Sheet (page 93) for the students

Procedure:

1. Collect an array of advertisements from print, TV, and Internet sources.

2. Discuss the meaning of assumption (i.e., unstated ideas or beliefs about someone or something).

3. Distribute several ads to each group of two to four students.

4. Suggest that each company, as it tries to sell its product, makes assumptions about buyers and what will motivate them to buy their product.

5. Provide an example, such as this one:

   An ad for shoes says, "Get fit this year with an exercise program that works for you. The first step in your new exercise program? Picking a fitness shoe that can keep up with you!"

Have each group discuss the assumptions the ad makes about the buyer. Remember to include any graphics found in the ad (e.g., the shoe ad features a happy woman jumping high, knees bent, with the "fitness shoes" on her feet). Ask students what is implied by the picture.

Assumptions for this ad might include:

- People want to exercise.
- They need special shoes to succeed in an exercise program.
- Shoes can make you jump high.
- Shoes can make you happy.
- Without special shoes, you will not be happy, successful, or able to jump high, etc.

6. Have each group fill out the Assumptions Activity Sheet for each product.
7. Have students share a selection of their examples in a discussion on assumptions.

Assumptions Activity Sheet

Name: _____ Date: _____

1. Company name: _____

    Ad statement: _____

    _____

    Assumption: _____

    _____

2. Company name: _____

    _____

    Ad statement: _____

    _____

    Assumption: _____

    _____

    Did any of the ads convince you—through words or pictures or the
assumptions behind them—that you should buy the product?   Why
or why not?

    _____

    _____

    _____

#50554—Information Literacy © Shell Education

Chapter 4

Organizing Information

We have established that images are powerful. Indeed, we take in most information through our eyes, and even text is a specialized form of visual information. So managing that information in pictorial or graphic form makes a lot of sense. Many students—those with strong spatial intelligence, for example—do a much better job of understanding and producing content when they can do so with images. For the purposes of this book, we will call everything that is not simple text an image. The term encompasses drawings, pictures, graphs, charts, storyboards, and other patterns and shapes with which information can be organized.

According to teachers Douglas Kipperman and Melissa McKinstry, who maintain the Write Design Online—Graphic Organizers website (**http://www.writedesignonline.com/organizers/index.html**), there are five kinds of graphic organizers:

1. A star or web shape that can lay out topics, concepts, or ideas.

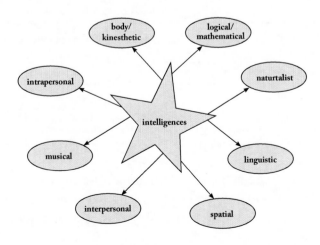

2. A chart or matrix that might list attributes for comparison, such as these few ideas that may start a discussion of evidence of student-centered and teacher-centered learning.

Student-centered Learning	Teacher-centered Learning
desks or work spaces in a circle or other flexible arrangement	desks or work spaces lined up and/or unmovable
content generated at least in part by students	content generated solely by textbooks
students become experts on topics	teacher is the only expert in the room
flexible time periods	district-mandated time periods

Venn diagrams also provide an interesting way to display information, particularly when comparing ideas or events that have overlapping areas.

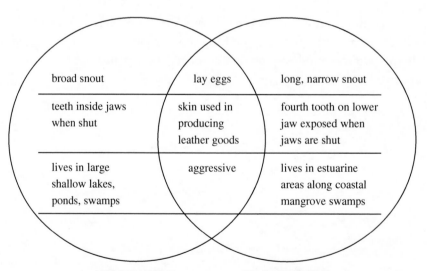

ALLIGATOR		CROCODILE
broad snout	lay eggs	long, narrow snout
teeth inside jaws when shut	skin used in producing leather goods	fourth tooth on lower jaw exposed when jaws are shut
lives in large shallow lakes, ponds, swamps	aggressive	lives in estuarine areas along coastal mangrove swamps

This diagram is based on information from "Alligators and Crocodiles," June 1991. Institute of Food and Agricultural Sciences, University of Florida, Gainesville 32611. **http://edis.ifas.ufl.edu/UW003**.

3. A tree or map that might allow for classifying or categorizing.

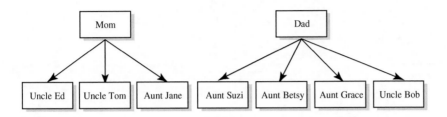

4. A chain that can show sequences of events in space or time.

5. Sketches or drawings that illustrate ideas.

A popular software program that helps students and teachers create graphic organizers is called *Inspiration*® (**http://www. inspiration.com**). For younger students, the company also makes *Kidspiration*®. In these programs, users are given many collections of shapes and pictures with which they can generate a wide range of pictorial layouts of information. The program also translates these layouts into outline form, if desired. And the layouts can be inserted into word-processing programs such as *Microsoft Word*®, as has been done in the first examples above and the sample on the following page.

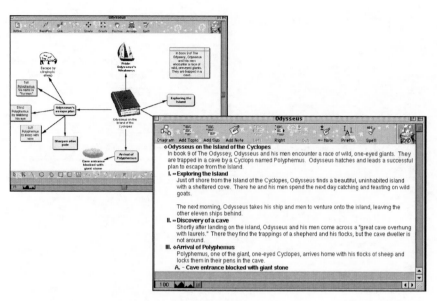

This diagram was created using *Inspiration*® by Inspiration Software, Inc.

In 2003, a study titled "Scientifically Based Research on Graphic Organizers" was completed by Inspiration Software, Inc., and the Institute for the Advancement of Research in Education (IARE). A summary and PDF of the full report can be found at **http://www.inspiration.com/resources/index.cfm?fuseaction=research**.

After looking at 29 studies on graphic organizers, researchers concluded the following:

> . . . *visual learning strategies improve student performance. Scientifically based research cited in the literature review demonstrates that a research base exists to support the use of graphic organizers for improving student learning and performance across grade levels, with diverse students, and in a broad range of content areas.* (p. 2)

IARE found that graphic organizers such as those described above help students improve in several areas, including reading comprehension (e.g., using story maps or layouts of sequences found in stories), thinking and learning skills (e.g., as a tool for brainstorming), and retention and recall of information (e.g., representing information in multiple ways), among others.

The study also looked at three cognitive learning theories and found that graphic organizers do indeed increase capacity for learning. The study explains that "three learning theories were reviewed that help to explain the 'why' and 'how' of what makes graphic organizers an important learning tool."

The three theories, according to the IARE study, are described as follows:

- Dual coding theory asserts that if individuals attend to both the nonverbal and verbal systems of processing information, the retention and recall of information is easier.

- Schema theory proposes that the use of a graphic organizer helps students link existing knowledge—organized in networks or schemas in our memories with new knowledge.

- Finally, cognitive load theory states working memory has a maximum capacity of information it can process. Graphic organizers can help reduce the cognitive load and, as a result, allow more of the working memory to attend to learning new material (p. 20).

Other examples of graphic organizers include cluster maps, decision trees, mind maps, concept maps, storyboards, sequence paths—any visual display that can support, enhance, or represent information. In addition to *Inspiration*® and *Kidspiration*®, you might also want to look at Cmap Tools (**http://cmap.ihmc.us/**), FreeMind (**http://freemind.sourceforge.net/wiki/index.php/Main_Page**), and Wikka Wiki (**http://wikkawiki.org/HomePage/**).

In traditional schools, students most often encounter letters and numbers. While it is important that all students read, write, and learn math, we all have at least eight intelligences (see the star diagram on page 95), according to Howard Gardner (*Frames of Mind*, Basic Books, 1983). Adding visual or graphical ways for students to learn material supports the possibility for intelligences other than linguistic and logical mathematical to come into play and increases opportunities for learning. For more information on Gardner's theory of multiple intelligences, see "I Think … Therefore … MI! Multiple Intelligences in Education" at **http://surfaquarium.com/MI/**, Howard Gardner, "Multiple Intelligences and Education" at **http://www.infed.org/thinkers/gardner.htm**, and "Concept to Classroom: Tapping into Multiple Intelligences" at **http://www.thirteen.org/edonline/concept2class/mi/index.html**.

A number of websites have been developed to support teachers' use of graphical organizers. The Graphic Organizer (**http://www.graphic.org/links.html**) will connect you to quite a few other sites, many of which include resources, examples, and research on the topic, as well as free trials of mind-mapping software and other commercial products.

Other sites include:

NCREL
http://www.ncrel.org/sdrs/areas/issues/students/learning/lr1grorg.htm

The North Central Regional Educational Laboratory has examples of a number of graphic organizers.

Graphic Organizers Links
http://www.nvo.com/ecnewletter/graphicorganizers/

This site is developed and maintained by Dee Ann Hill, an educator in Fort Worth, Texas. It is quite extensive, with many links and other materials and information for parents, teachers, and students.

4 Blocks Literacy Framework: Graphic Organizers
http://www.k111.k12.il.us/lafayette/fourblocks/graphic_organizers.htm

Four Blocks Literacy Framework, developed by Pat Cunningham and Dottie Hall of Wake Forest University, is a "multimethod, multilevel literacy framework," according to its authors.

ERIC Graphic Organizers: Elementary School
http://www.indiana.edu/~reading/ieo/bibs/graphele.html

ERIC Graphic Organizers: Secondary School

http://www.indiana.edu/~reading/ieo/bibs/graphsec.html

These two sites were put together by Ping-Yun Sun, reference specialist for the ERIC Clearinghouse on reading, English, and communication. They contain links to a few sites, a compilation of ERIC citations on the topic, and other resources as well.

Activity: Graphic Organizer Practice

Introduction:

Graphic organizers can allow students to expand their spatial intelligences and organize their questions graphically. By laying out information in a chart, in a sequence of boxes, or in a star, tree, or web shape, students can identify different ways to organize information other than outlines or other hierarchical text formats.

You may want to visit one or more of the websites listed on the previous page, particularly Write Design Online: Graphic Organizers (**http://www.writedesignonline.com/organizers/index.html**) and NCREL (**http://www.ncrel.org/sdrs/areas/issues/students/learning/lr1grorg.htm**). In these sites, you can acquaint yourself with a number of layouts. You may also want to develop a few examples using *Inspiration*® or *Kidspiration*® (see **http://www.inspiration.com/resources/index.cfm** for examples and ideas in curriculum areas).

Objectives:

- Students will learn about a variety of graphic organizers.
- Students will use a graphic organizer to lay out their research for a project.
- Students will increase their understanding of developing good questions within a graphic organizer.

Materials:

- paper and pen, or a computer with graphic organizer software installed

Procedure:

1. Ask students to brainstorm questions and areas they will address in a project.
2. Suggest that students develop a K-W-L-H chart as a start and

recall the types of questions they might want to focus on for their project.

3. Students draw their K-W-L-H charts and then build another layout or develop a layout online using software such as *Inspiration*® or *Kidspiration*®, as they identify the areas and questions they will research.

4. Students share their layouts with a partner who will provide feedback on the areas of exploration and depth of questions.

5. Students then write a response to the comments and suggestions they received, and incorporate them into their layouts. The layouts and responses are turned in to the teacher, who approves the work and thus gives the go-ahead for the project, or asks for more information or corrections before work can proceed.

6. After everyone has had a chance to develop a graphic organizer, conduct a class discussion about the benefits and drawbacks of using graphic organizers rather than simply writing up a proposal for a project. Poll the groups for the kinds of organizers they used (e.g., cluster diagrams, charts) so that everyone can become more familiar with the types available.

Reflection:

As students become more familiar with graphic organizers both on and off the computer, continued discussions about when to use them and for what purposes will be beneficial. Helping students realize which techniques and tools they find successful for learning is a continual process.

Activity: Storyboard

Introduction:

Storyboards are used by filmmakers to prepare for shooting a film. This organizational tool can be used for any project. Using a storyboard helps students organize their thinking, plan out a piece of writing or a project, and see how the parts of a multimedia project will fit together.

Objectives:

- Students will create a storyboard for a writing assignment that includes illustrations.

Materials:

- four-by-six-inch cards for each student, colored markers, access to a computer with a word-processing program, chart paper or colored construction paper

Procedure:

1. Introduce the idea of storyboards. Brainstorm with students different people who might use this graphic organizer (e.g., filmmakers, cartoonists).

2. Discuss a writing assignment with students. Let them know that they will be asked to write a story of their choosing and then illustrate it.

3. Have students use four-by-six-inch cards to organize their writing. Instruct students to outline their stories on cards, putting different parts of the story on each card. This can take the place of outlining, and students have the benefit of being able to move the cards around to see if different sequences of the story flow better than others.

4. Explain to students that they will use their cards to write their stories, which should be about one and a half to two pages long.

The topic can be of their own choosing or directly related to a language arts or social studies topic that the class is studying.

5. Have students work with partners to edit and revise their stories. Students should come up with a final draft that has been word-processed. Make sure students use at least 14-point type and leave several lines of space between paragraphs.

6. When the stories are ready, explain that students will use more four-by-six-inch cards to draw illustrations or mount photos they have taken to illustrate their stories. The easiest way to do this is to have students lay out the cards with a word or two on each to indicate where the illustration will go in the text.

7. Have students work with partners to check the layout and flow of their stories and illustrations.

8. Have students cut their text so that paragraphs or sections of the story are separate from each other.

9. Have students arrange the cards with illustrations in the sequence they want, and then align the illustrations with their corresponding text sections.

10. Students can mount these stories on chart paper or colored construction paper. If you like, they can retype their stories so that each section of text measures four inches by six inches to match the cards on which their illustrations have been placed.

11. After the students share their stories with the class, you may want to display them in the school hallway, have your students share their stories with younger students, or make a book of the mounted stories for the classroom.

Reflection:

This activity will begin to prepare students for multimedia projects in which graphics, images, sound, text, and transitional elements will be brought together to produce a short video or digital story.

Chapter 5

Where Did That Come From?

Wherever information comes from, someone created it. It's true that ideas are free and cannot be copyrighted, but any manifestation of an idea—a book, a website, a piece of artwork—can be protected because it belongs to someone. Students will agree that if they were to find out that someone else was using their hard work regardless of whether credit was given, they might feel that they had been treated unfairly. Modeling good habits early in terms of teaching students about copyright and fair use, as well as how to properly cite where they find information, will help them tremendously on their path toward becoming critical thinkers and users and creators of information. In this chapter, some of the issues related to copyright, fair use, and citing sources are addressed with an eye toward helping students think about where information comes from, how they might use it, and the ethical considerations involved in doing so.

Copyright

Stanford University Libraries (**http://fairuse.stanford.edu**) have created an extensive website that addresses many topics relating to copyright and fair use through a number of links and online materials. For example, the Copyright Web Sites page (**http://fairuse.stanford. edu/web_resources/web_sites.html**) links to more than 75 sites that cover copyright law, intellectual property, national and international applications, and digital and electronic media.

The U.S. Copyright Office (**http://www.copyright.gov**) also provides information, including how to search for copyrights and how to register a copyright on your original work.

As we work with students, it seems safest to assume that someone owns any material students come across from any medium, and if students want to use it, they must at least cite their sources. (See below for a fuller discussion of this topic, as well as citation guidelines.)

However, there is some leeway in two areas: noncopyright-protected materials (including U.S. government documents) and fair use in education.

According to the U.S. Copyright Office, there are a number of things that cannot be copyright protected, and therefore no permission is needed for their use. For example:

- works that have not been fixed in a tangible form of expression (e.g., choreographic works that have not been notated or recorded, or improvisational speeches or performances that have not been written or recorded)

- titles, names, short phrases, and slogans; familiar symbols or designs; mere variations of typographic ornamentation, lettering, or coloring; mere listings of ingredients or contents

- ideas, procedures, methods, systems, processes, concepts, principles, discoveries, or devices, as distinguished from a description, explanation, or illustration

- works consisting entirely of information that is common property and containing no original authorship (e.g., standard calendars, height and weight charts, tape measures and rulers, and lists or tables taken from public documents or other common sources)

These four items were taken directly from the U.S. Copyright Office website, "Copyright Office Basics: What Is Not Protected by Copyright?" at **http://www.copyright.gov/circs/circ1.html#wnp**.

Fair Use

The following document from the U.S. Copyright Office reveals current views on fair use of copyrighted material.

One of the rights accorded to the owner of a copyright is the right to reproduce or to authorize others to reproduce the work in copies or phono records. This right is subject to certain limitations found in Sections 107 through 118 of the Copyright Act (title 17, U.S. Code). One of the more important limitations is the doctrine of fair use. Although fair use was not mentioned in the previous copyright law, the doctrine has developed through a substantial number of court decisions over the years. This doctrine has been codified in Section 107 of the copyright law.

Section 107 contains a list of the various purposes for which the reproduction of a particular work may be considered "fair," such as criticism, comment, news reporting, teaching, scholarship, and research. Section 107 also sets out four factors to be considered in determining whether a particular use is fair:

- the purpose and character of the use, including whether such use is of commercial nature or is for nonprofit educational purposes
- the nature of the copyrighted work
- the amount and substantiality of the portion used in relation to the copyrighted work as a whole
- the effect of the use upon the potential market for or value of the copyrighted work

The distinction between fair use and infringement may be unclear and not easily defined. There is no specific number of words, lines, or notes that may safely be taken without permission. Acknowledging the source of the copyrighted material does not substitute for obtaining permission.

The 1961 Report of the Register of Copyrights on the General Revision of the U.S. Copyright Law cites examples of activities that courts have regarded as fair use: "quotation of excerpts in a review or criticism for purposes of illustration or comment; quotation of short passages in a scholarly or technical work for illustration or clarification of the author's observations; use in a parody of some of the content of the work parodied; summary of an address or article, with brief quotations, in a news report; reproduction by a library of a portion of a work to replace part of a damaged copy; reproduction by a teacher or student of a small part of a work to illustrate a lesson; reproduction of a work in legislative or judicial proceedings or reports; incidental and fortuitous reproduction, in a newsreel or broadcast, of a work located in the scene of an event being reported."

Copyright protects the particular way an author has expressed himself or herself; it does not extend to any ideas, systems, or factual information conveyed in the work.

The safest course is always to get permission from the copyright owner before using copyrighted material. The Copyright Office cannot give this permission.

When it is impracticable to obtain permission, use of copyrighted material should be avoided unless the doctrine of fair use would clearly apply to the situation. The Copyright Office can neither determine if a certain use may be considered "fair" nor advise on possible copyright violations. If there is any doubt, it is advisable to consult an attorney. (FL-102, Revised July 2006. **http://www.copyright.gov/fls/fl102.html**)

Creative Commons

A fascinating new development in copyright can be found in Creative Commons (**http://creativecommons.org/**). This nonprofit group strives to find a middle ground between those who want total control over their work and those who are totally open about their work. The middle ground can be sharing your work with some range of restrictions attached. Creative Commons lists six possible licenses:

Attribution Noncommercial No Derivatives means your work may be downloaded and shared, but not changed, and must link back and credit you.

Attribution Noncommercial Share Alike means others may take your work, add to it, change it, etc., but must attribute the original to you and license the new work under the same terms.

Attribution Noncommercial means others may take your work and make derivative works but must acknowledge you. They do not have to license their work in the same way. However, the works must be licensed under one of the noncommercial licenses.

Attribution No Derivatives means others may use your work but may not change it, and must attribute it to you.

Attribution Share Alike means others may take your work and change it, add to it, etc., but must license the new work under the same terms—for commercial or noncommercial use.

Attribution (by) means others may take your work and do anything they want with it as long as you are credited.

By making one's work available under a Creative Commons license, it becomes more widely accessible and remains a living thing, as the majority of the Creative Commons licenses allow others to build upon the original. The dynamism inherent in these licenses acknowledges the original intent of the Internet as a place where sharing and learning take place. We all win when we share our work and build on the work of others.

Media literacy is not just about becoming smarter media users, but is also about becoming creative, flexible media creators.

—Bertram C. Bruce (2003)

The Educator's Guide to Copyright and Fair Use

By Hall Davidson

This is the way it happens: You're a teacher. You find the perfect resource for a lesson you're building for your class. It's a picture from the Internet, or a piece of a song, or a page or two from a book in the library or from your own collection. There's no time to ask for permission from who owns it. There isn't even time to figure who or what exactly does own it. You use the resource anyway, and then you worry. Have you violated copyright law? What kind of example are you setting for students?

Or you're the principal. You visit a classroom and see an outstanding lesson that involves videotape, or an MP3 audio file from the Web, or photocopies from a book you know your school doesn't own. Do you make a comment?

The Original Intent

Were the framers of the Constitution or the barons of old English law able to look over your shoulder, they would be puzzled by your doubts because all of the above uses are legal. Intellectual property was created to promote the public good. In old England, if you wanted to copyright a book, you gave copies to the universities. According to Supreme Court Justice Sandra Day O'Connor, "The primary objective of copyright is not to reward the labor of authors ... but encourage others to build freely upon the ideas and information conveyed by a work." In other words, copyright was created to benefit society at large, not to protect commercial interests.

Nowhere is this statement truer than in the educational arena. In fact, educators fall under a special category under the law known as "fair use." The concept, which first formally appeared in the 1976 Copyright Act, allows certain groups to use intellectual property deemed to benefit society as a whole (e.g., in schools for instructional use). However, it deliberately did not spell out the details. Over the years, fair use guidelines have been created by a number of groups—usually a combination of educators, intellectual-property holders, and other interested parties.

These are not actual laws but widely accepted "deals" the educational community and companies have struck and expect each other to follow.

What follows is a new version of "The Educators' Lean and Mean No FAT Guide to Fair Use," published in *Technology & Learning* magazine several years ago. As you take the Copyright Quiz (pages 115–117), you will learn that no matter the technology—photocopying, downloading, file sharing, video duplication—there are times when copying is not only acceptable, it is encouraged for the purposes of teaching and learning. And you will learn that the rights are strongest and longest at the place where educators need them most: in the classroom. However, schools need to monitor and enforce fair use. If they don't, as the Los Angeles Unified School District found out in a six-figure settlement, they may find themselves on the losing end of a copyright question.

Know Your Limitations—and Rights

It has never been a more important time to know the rules. As a result of laws written and passed by Congress, companies are now creating technologies that block users from fair use of intellectual property. For example, teachers can't pull DVD files into video projects, and some computers now block users from inputting VCRs and other devices. In addition to helping schools steer clear of legal trouble, understanding the principles of fair use will allow educators to aggressively pursue new areas where technology and learning are ahead of the law, and to speak out when they feel their rights to copyright material have been violated.

Now take a quiz that will assess your knowledge of what is allowable—and what isn't—under fair use copyright principles and guidelines. There's also a handy chart that outlines teachers' fair use rights and responsibilities. Good luck.

Davidson is director of the Discovery Education Network and director of the California Student Media Festival (**http://www. mediafestival.org/**). He can be reached at hhdavidson@sbcglobal. net or **http://www.halldavidson.org**, where you will also find other materials and information.

Activity: The Copyright Quiz

Answer true or false to the following 20 questions.

Part I: Computers and Software

1. A student snaps in half a CD-ROM the teacher really needed for her next class. The teacher decides to make backup copies of all her crucial disks so it never happens again. It is permissible for her to do this. T_____ F_____

2. A technology coordinator installs the one copy of *Adobe Photoshop*® the school owns on a central server so students are able to access it from their classroom workstations. This is a violation of copyright law. T_____ F_____

3. A school has a site license for version 3.3 of a multimedia program. A teacher buys five copies of version 4.0, which is more powerful, and installs them on five workstations in the computer lab. But now when students at these workstations create a project and bring it back to their classrooms, the computers running version 3.3 won't read the work! To end the chaos, it's permissible to install version 4.0 on all machines. T_____ F_____

4. The state mandates technology proficiency for all high school students but adds no money to schools' software budgets. To ensure equity, public schools are allowed to buy what software they can afford and copy the rest. T_____ F_____

5. A geography teacher has more students and computers than software. He uses a CD burner to make several copies of a copyrighted interactive CD-ROM so each student can use an individual copy in class. This is fair use. T_____ F_____

Part II: The Internet

6. A middle school science class studying ocean ecosystems must gather material for multimedia projects. The teacher downloads pictures of and information on marine life from various commercial and noncommercial sites to store in a folder for students to access. This is fair use. T_____ F____

7. An elementary school designs a password-protected website for families and faculty only. It's okay for teachers to post student work on the site. T_____ F_____

8. A student film buff downloads a new release from a Taiwanese website to use for a humanities project. As long as the student gives credit to the sites from which he's downloaded material, this is covered under fair use. T_____ F_____

9. A technology coordinator downloads audio clips from MP3.com to integrate into a curriculum project. This is fair use. T_____ F_____

10. A teacher gets clip art and music from popular file-sharing sites, creates a lesson plan, and posts it on the school website to share with other teachers. This is permissible. T_____ F_____

Part III: Video

11. A teacher videotapes a rerun of *Frontier House*, the PBS reality show that profiles three modern families living as homesteaders from the 1880s. In class, students edit themselves "into" the frontier and make fun of the spoiled family from California. This is fair use. T_____ F_____

12. A student tries to digitize the shower scene from a rented copy of *Psycho* into a "History of Horror" report. Her computer won't do it. The movie happens to be on an NBC TV station that week, so the teacher tapes it and then digitizes it on the computer for her. This is fair use. T_____ F_____

13. A history class videotapes a Holocaust survivor who lives in the community. The students digitally compress the interview and, with the interviewee's permission, post it on the Web. Another school discovers the interview online and uses it in its History Day project. This is fair use. T_____ F_____

14. On back-to-school night, an elementary school offers childcare for students' younger siblings. They put the kids in the library and show them Disney VHS tapes bought by the PTA. This is permissible. T_____ F_____

15. A teacher makes a compilation of movie clips from various VHS tapes to use in his classroom as lesson starters. This is covered under fair use. T_____ F_____

Part IV: Multimedia

16. At a local electronics show, a teacher buys a machine that defeats the copy protection on DVDs, CD-ROMs, and just about everything else. She lets her students use it so they can incorporate clips from rented DVDs into their film-genre projects. This is fair use. T_____ F_____

17. A number of students take digital pictures of local streets and businesses for their Web projects. These are permissible to post online. T_____ F_____

18. A student wants to play a clip of ethnic music to represent her family's country of origin. Her teacher has a CD-ROM that meets her needs. It is fair use for the student to copy and use the music in her project. T_____ F_____

19. A high school video class produces a DVD yearbook that includes the year's top 10 music hits as background music. This is fair use. T_____ F_____

20. Last year, a school's science fair multimedia CD-ROM was so popular that everyone wanted a copy of it. Everything in it was copied under fair use guidelines. It's permissible for the school to sell copies to recover the costs of reproduction. T_____ F_____

The Copyright Quiz can be downloaded as a PDF from the Tech & Learning website at **http://www.techlearning.com/techlearning/ pdf/events/techforum/tx05/2002TLQuiz.pdf** and is used here with permission. Or, view the quiz online at **http://www.techlearning. com/db_area/archives/TL/2002/10/copyright_quiz.php**.

The Copyright Quiz with answers can be found online at **http://www.techlearning.com/db_area/archives/TL/2002/10/ copyright_answers.php.**

See pages 227–229 for the answers!

Also, check out the Resources section for a copy of Davidson's Copyright and Fair Use Guidelines for Teachers chart (page 230), reprinted with permission from *Technology & Learning* magazine. The updated two-page copyright chart can be downloaded in PDF format from Davidson's website: **http://halldavidson.org/downloads.html#anchor923173**.

Activity: Student Copyright Scenarios

Introduction:

Since it is so easy to copy information, everyone is doing it, right? Students may not have considered copyright and fair use practices when they downloaded music, movies, and other information, although there has been much discussion in the media for a number of years. In these scenarios, students will consider and discuss what is right—legally and ethically.

Objectives:

- Students will encounter challenging copyright dilemmas.
- Students will review copyright information.
- Students will share their thoughts and findings.

Materials:

- copies of copyright scenarios (pages 121–122) for the students, Internet access, any print materials having to do with copyright

Procedure:

1. Lead the class in a discussion of copyright dos and don'ts.
2. Tell students they will be working in groups to consider some cases that have to do with copyright practices. They will work as a group to come to agreement about how to handle each scenario.
3. After students have discussed the scenarios and come to agreement, lead a class discussion on their decisions and the reasoning behind them.

Reflection:

By engaging students in conversations about real-world situations in which they may find themselves, they will better understand copyright practices and, we hope, at least question their own actions when their use of copyrighted work may be an issue.

Copyright Scenarios

Scenario 1:

You were given a CD for your birthday and love what you hear. Since it was a gift (someone purchased it) and you actually have the CD in your hand, it is legal to make copies for your friends. True or false? Why or why not?

Scenario 2:

You download music from your favorite website and transfer the songs to another device. Since you will only be listening to it on one device at a time, this is legal. True or false? Why or why not?

Scenario 3:

You have a presentation due on causes of the Civil War. There is lots of information online, and you read a lot and copy a lot but put everything into your own words in your presentation. Everything goes well until the teacher marks you down because you did not list every source of your information. Fair or not fair? Why or why not?

Scenario 4:

Your teacher gives you a disk containing open-source software programs. There is great content here, such as a good word processor, a mind-mapping program, an art program, and more. She says you can take it home, load it onto as many machines as you want, and share it with friends. This is legal. True or false? Why or why not?

Scenario 5:

You and your friends think that adding music to a successful presentation and sharing it with friends and family in decorated copies is a great idea. In fact, everyone loves what you have done so much that they want copies to give to others and are willing to pay for you to make copies. This is legal. True or false? Why or why not?

Scenario 6:

You find a piece of music that you really like, which you download. You think you can make it better by overlaying your own drum accompaniment. You upload the new version to share with anyone who wants it. You notice the original piece carries a Creative Commons Attribution Non-commercial Share Alike license. What do you have to do to make sure what you have done is legal?

Student teams will want to consult the U.S. Copyright website (**http://www.www.copyright.gov**), a source citation site such as Son of Citation Machine (**http://citationmachine.net/?resize=1**), and the Creative Commons site (**http://www.creativecommons.org**).

Citing Sources

Information abounds and is available to teachers and students. Often, we do not even need to ask permission to use it. However, an important practice to follow at all times is to require students to cite their sources. Rather than appear to diminish us as thinkers, writers, and speakers, citing sources reveals our breadth of exploration and the range of ideas we considered as we formulated our understanding of a topic.

There are two common styles in which to cite sources: Modern Language Association (MLA) and American Psychological Association (APA). The former style is often used in education and literary works, while the latter is often used in writing for the social sciences.

On the MLA website (**http://www.mla.org**), you might want to look at the Frequently Asked Questions about MLA Style section for answers to specific questions about citations: **http://www.mla.org/publications/style/style_faq/**.

On the APA website (**http://www.apa.org**), the APA Style Guide section provides details on using this style: **http://www.apastyle.apa.org/**. You may also want to take a look at the Frequently Asked Questions section of this site as well: **http://www.apastyle.org/faqs.html**.

The citations themselves contain the same information, but may be arranged or emphasized differently. For example, see how the citation for a book I edited, *Snapshots! Educational Insights from the Thornburg Center*, would appear in the two formats:

MLA Style:

Armstrong, Sara, ed. *Snapshots! Educational Insights from the Thornburg Center*. Chicago: Starsong, 2003.

APA Style:

Armstrong, S. (Ed.). (2003). *Snapshots! Educational Insights from the Thornburg Center*. Chicago: Starsong.

The most important point is to identify the details of the source of information, pick a style, be consistent, and provide enough information so that the reader can find out more about the source that was used.

Because of increasing access to a variety of sources on the Internet, guidelines for citing sources have increased. A very fine tool for students is available at David Warlick's Landmarks for Schools website (**http://www.landmark-project.com/index.php**). Warlick created the Citation Machine and made it freely available. Now, Son of Citation Machine is available for students to use to cite sources using MLA, APA, Turabian, or Chicago styles (**http://citationmachine. net/?resize=1**).

If your students need to cite books by single or multiple authors, websites, articles, interviews, or email postings, all they have to do is fill in the online form, and the machine will provide the citation in the style they have chosen, which is how I got the citations for my book.

The picture below was taken from the website (with permission) and shows the first step in the process.

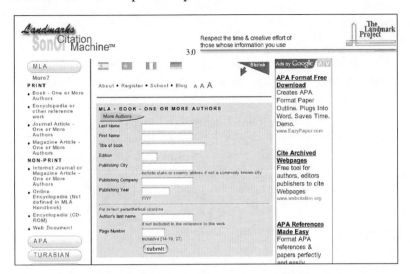

I clicked on MLA and chose Book—one or more authors as the kind of source I was citing, and a template came up into which I inputted the book's information.

The result can be entered into any word-processing program and should be repeated for all sources used in a project.

This is one example of a site that makes it easy for students to cite sources. We should make sure our students give credit for any information they use. After all, they will be pleased to be cited when others quote their hard work on the Web, in articles, and in presentations.

Activity: Who You Gonna Call?

Introduction:

While it is not necessary to ask permission to use information from a website in many educational situations, it is important that students know how to obtain permission if they need it—and know when they need to ask. In this activity, students will visit a variety of websites and ascertain whether they need permission and, if so, who should be contacted for permission to use materials from the site. Students will also draft a letter to be sent to one of the sources as if they were asking for permission.

Objectives:

- Students will review websites for contact information.
- Students will develop a permission request letter for website information.

Materials:

- board for recording student ideas, paper and pencils, copies of the Permission Request Activity Sheet (pages 129–130) for each student

Procedure:

1. Talk with students about the importance of citing sources and having permission to use material from a website in their reports or projects.
2. Solicit ideas from students about requesting permission, including how they would go about it (e.g., letter, phone call, email), what they would ask, etc.
3. Let students know they will work in teams, visit up to six sites on the Internet, and record information on their activity sheets about each site and how they might get permission to use it. (You may

want to have students go to just a few of these sites, or have students identify sites they have used or will use for projects and reports and find the contact information for them.) Generally, there will be information at the bottom of a page or in the "Contact Us" section about where to go for permission. Sometimes, individual authors or artists will be listed as copyright holders with their contact information.

4. When most teams have completed this part of the assignment, hold a discussion in which students talk about their experiences: Was it hard to find someone to contact? Was the contact information complete? What do students conclude about a website that does not provide clear contact information?

5. Ask students to choose one of the sites they identified. Tell them they will be drafting a letter to send to that website, asking permission for its use.

6. Ask students what information should be included in a letter (or email) that is asking permission. Write student ideas on the board.

7. Decide together on the items that need to be included in the letters the students will write. Be sure to include the following: name and contact information of the person requesting permission, a specific statement of what is being asked for (text and/or images), the URL, the purpose of the use, the time frame in which the permission is needed, an assurance that the material will be properly cited, and a thank you. Very comprehensive examples of student and teacher request forms can be found at the Landmark Schools website: **http://www.landmark-project.com/permission1.php**. However, there is value in helping students think through the request process on their own.

8. Continue discussions with students about the need to ask for permission to use materials from other media and the differences among media. For example, information in books and magazines can be thought about, synthesized, and incorporated into student reports and projects without asking permission. But using images and text from websites or reusing photographs requires permission.

Reflection:

You may want students to keep track of the websites they have researched in an Internet journal or notebook. When reviewing websites for projects and reports, students may want to fill out a simple evaluation page for each site, including the name of the site, URL, what it might be used for, and whether permission is needed for its use. Contact information for whoever grants permission could be included as well. These forms could be compiled in a class notebook. Then, students would have their own sources of online references they might use for their future work.

Permission Request Activity Sheet

Name: _____ Date: _____

On this activity sheet, record contact information for the following six websites.

1. If you wanted to include the "Optical Illusion: Which Is Tallest?" science experiment from the National Geographic Kids website in a project you were working on, would you need to ask permission, and if so, whom would you contact for permission? **http://www.nationalgeographic.com/ngkids/trythis/tryoptical5.html**

    _____

2. If you wanted to use the picture of the Mars Rover from the Exploratorium website, would you need to ask permission, and if so, whom would you contact for permission? **http://www.exploratorium.edu/mars/rovers.html**

    _____

3. If you wanted to use a picture from the Louvre website of the famous painting "Mona Lisa," would you need to ask for permission to use it? If so, whom would you contact for the permission? **http://www.louvre.fr/llv/contacts/liste_contacts.jsp?bmLocale=en**

    _____

4. If you wanted to use the story "The Merman's Sock" from the Stories for the Seasons website, would you need to ask permission, and if so, whom would you contact for permission? **http://www.h-net.org/~nilas/seasons/**

    _____

5. If you wanted to use some pictures of monarch butterflies from the Journey North website, would you need to ask permission, and if so, whom would you contact for permission? **http://www.learner.org/jnorth/**

_____

6. If you wanted to use a picture of J. K. Rowling from the _Harry Potter_ author's site at Scholastic Books, would you need to ask permission, and if so, whom would you contact for permission? **http://www.scholastic.com/harrypotter/author/index.htm**

_____

Activity: Citing Sources

Introduction:

Helping students understand why and how to acknowledge information they find from a variety of sources is critical. In this activity, students will work with a variety of sources and learn to cite them using either MLA or APA style.

Objectives:

- Students will learn about MLA and APA styles.

- Students will learn to cite a variety of sources using the Citing Sources Activity Sheets.

- Students will contribute to a class book (hard copy or online) made up of examples of citations for all the different types of information sources they will need for a variety of projects and assignments.

Materials:

- a range of materials to be cited (e.g., books; anthologies; online journal articles; magazines; newspapers; interviews; emails; Web pages; encyclopedias, both print and CD; broadcast programs); examples of MLA and APA style citations; copies for each student of the Citing Sources Activity Sheet—MLA Style (pages 134–135), and/or the Citing Sources Activity Sheet—APA Style (pages 136–137)

- Optional: a set of printed Citation Machine templates for information sources in the style you will be using. These can be easily made by entering citation information into the Son of Citation Machine found at David Warlick's website: **http://citationmachine.net/?resize=1**.

Procedure:

1. Begin a discussion on the importance of citing sources. Ask students why they think they should include citations in their work.

2. Introduce students to the idea of two styles of citation. Provide examples of citations for books, magazine articles, websites, and emails in both formats. These could be reproduced on cards, if desired. For example:

   ### Books

   MLA:

   Rowling, J. K. *Harry Potter and the Deathly Hallows*. New York: Scholastic Books, 2007.

   APA:

   Rowling, J. (2007). *Harry Potter and the deathly hallows*. New York, NY: Scholastic Books.

   ### Magazine articles

   MLA:

   Rigby, Ken, and Bruce Johnson. "Playground Heroes." *Greater Good* (2006–07): 14–17.

   APA:

   Rigby, Ken, & Johnson, Bruce (2006–07). Playground heroes. *Greater good*. 14–17.

   ### Websites

   MLA:

   "Yahoo! Kids" Yahoo! Inc. 04 Jan. 2008, **http://kids. yahoo.com**.

   APA:

   Yahoo Kids. Retrieved Jan. 4, 2008, **http://kids.yahoo. com**.

Email

MLA:

Armstrong, Sara. (saarmst@telis.org). "Winter Class Project." Email to Kirby Jackson (kjackson@somewhere. com). 04 January 2008.

APA:

Do not include in reference list; cite in text only.

3. Ask students why they think there are differences between the two styles, particularly with regard to the email citations.

4. Let students know which style you will be using in your class. (You will find two versions of the Citing Sources Activity Sheet: one filled out in MLA style and the other in APA style.)

5. Have students work in pairs or small groups, and assign types of citations they will develop using the Citing Sources Activity Sheet. That is, no one will prepare all 14 citations. Perhaps you want each student to learn about and create three to five citations, so the pairs or small groups can identify which among the 14 they will work on. Or, you can assign specific information sources to each pair or small group, ensuring that all information sources will be researched and that the class will then have examples of each.

6. Bring students together when the assignment is completed, and solicit their thoughts about citing different kinds of sources.

Reflection:

Ask students to reflect on different citation styles and comment on the information they think should or should not be included for a citation to be complete.

Citing Sources Activity Sheet—MLA Style

Name: _____ Date: _____

    Select the sources that you will be using in your class to practive citing in the MLA style. You may make notes of the information you will need to enter into the Son of Citation Machine (**http://citationmachine.net/?resize=1**). Refer to the website or the class set of printed templates for the items you will need for your citations.

1. book (single author):

   Example: Author's last name, comma, author's first name and initial, if any, followed by a period. Name of the book underlined, followed by a period. City in which the book was published, followed by a colon. Name of the publisher, followed by a comma, year in which the book was published, followed by a period. Rowling, J. K. *Harry Potter and the Deathly Hallows*. New York: Scholastic Books, 2007.

2. book (multiple authors): _____

   _____

3. book (editor): _____

   _____

4. article or chapter in an anthology: _____

   _____

5. journal article: _____

   _____

6. online journal article: _____

   _____

7. newspaper article: _____

   _____

8. online newspaper article: _____

9. interview: _____

10. email message: _____

11. Web page: _____

12. encyclopedia article (book): _____

13. encyclopedia article (CD-ROM): _____

14. broadcast program: _____

List any other sources of information you can think of and prepare citations you think would meet the standards of the MLA style. For example, how would you cite a video game?

_____

_____

_____

_____

_____

_____

_____

_____

Prepare a short report that includes the citations you were asked to make, along with your original citation ideas.

Citing Sources Activity Sheet—APA Style

Name: _____ Date: _____

    Select the sources that you will be using in your class to practive citing in the APA style. You may make notes of the information you will need to enter into the Son of Citation Machine (**http:// citationmachine.net/?resize=1**). Refer to the website or the class set of printed templates for the items you will need for your citations.

1. book (single author):

   <u>Example: Author's last name, comma, the first letter of the author's first name, followed by a period. The date of the publication in parentheses, followed by a period. Name of the book in italics, followed by a period. City in which the book is published, followed by a comma and the initials of the state, followed by a colon. Name of the publisher, followed by a period. Rowling, J. (2007). *Harry Potter and the Deathly Hallows*. New York, NY: Scholastic Books.</u>

2. book (multiple authors): _____

   _____

3. book (editor): _____

   _____

4. article or chapter in an anthology: _____

   _____

5. journal article: _____

   _____

6. online journal article: _____

   _____

7. newspaper article: _____

   _____

8. online newspaper article: _____

_____

9. interview: _____

_____

10. email message: _____

_____

11. Web page: _____

_____

12. encyclopedia article (book): _____

_____

13. encyclopedia article (CD-ROM): _____

_____

14. broadcast program: _____

List any other sources of information you can think of and prepare citations you think would meet the standards of the APA style. For example, how would you cite a video game?

_____

_____

_____

_____

_____

_____

_____

Prepare a short report that includes the citations you were asked to make, along with your original citation ideas.

Chapter 6

Search Techniques and Strategies

There is a lot of information available on the Internet. However, all of us have had frustrating and fruitless search experiences. Bernie Dodge, Ph.D., father of WebQuests, has developed some strategies for successful searching.

Four NETS for Better Searching

By Bernie Dodge, Ph.D.

http://webquest.sdsu.edu/searching/fournets.htm

The perfect page is out there somewhere. It's the page that has exactly the information you're looking for, and to you, it's beautiful and unattainable like a faraway star. If only you had a supersized net for capturing it!

Most people use a search engine by simply typing a few words into the query box and then scrolling through whatever comes up. Sometimes their choice of words ends up narrowing the search unduly, preventing them from finding what they're looking for. More often the end result of the search is a haystack of off-target Web pages that must be combed through. You can do better than that, and that's what this page is about.

The most comprehensive search engine out there at the moment seems to be Google, and that's what we'll focus on here. The first step in becoming a facile catcher of Web pages is to master Google's Advanced Search form located at **http://www.google.com/advanced_search**. Bookmark it! Drag the bookmark to your browser's toolbar so that it's always available.

If you make a habit of using the four techniques described below, you'll be a much better searcher than 90 percent of all Web users. It's just four things, and each will provide you with a better net for catching information.

Net 1: Start Narrow

The biggest problem people have with search engines (perhaps) is that they're so good! You can type in a word and within a fraction of a second, you'll have 20,000 pages to look at. Most of those pages will not be exactly what you're after, and you have to spend a load of time wading through the 19,993 that aren't quite right.

If you know what you're after, why not start by asking for it as precisely as you can?

Think of all the words that would always appear on the perfect page. Put those in the "all these words" field.

Think of all the distracting pages that might also turn up because one or more of your search terms has multiple meanings. What words can you think of that might help you eliminate those pages? Put those in the "any of these unwanted words" field.

If there's a term with synonyms, either of which might appear on the page you're after, put them in the "one or more of these words" field.

Try each of the searches now, and record how many sites you find.

As you do each search, take note of what kinds of sites turn up. Notice that the more specific the terms you include and exclude, the more focused your search.

Query	# of Matches
Imagine that you're interested in the legendary lost continent of *Atlantis*. There have been several movies with Atlantis in the title, but you're not interested in them. You are also not interested in the space shuttle *Atlantis*. Try this search: All these words: Atlantis continent Without the words: shuttle film movie	Write the number of hits you get below.
Here's how to search for it poorly: With all of the words: Atlantis	
Here's another search to try: All these words: Waterbury One or more of these words: Vermont VT Any of these unwanted words: Connecticut CT	
Here's how to search for Waterbury, VT, poorly: All these words: Waterbury	

Net 2: Find Exact Phrases

Words hang together in predictable ways. If you type a phrase into the "this exact wording or phrase" field in Google, you'll be able to locate pages in which those words appear together in that order. This is obviously useful for finding things that have a proper name consisting of several words (e.g., places, book titles, people).

It's also useful when you can remember a distinctive phrase from something you've read, but now need to locate it. What's the rest of the poem that starts with "Jenny kissed me when we met"?

The ability to search for phrases can be surprisingly useful. Do you suspect that something your student turned in was plagiarized or at least heavily borrowed without attribution? Type in a phrase or two from the paper and see if it turns up elsewhere. You can also check to see if your own work is being copied without your permission.

Another use for this feature: stamping out urban legends. Next time you get an email warning you about a repressive new law about to pass or a vicious computer virus about to attack, check it out before passing on misinformation to others. Type in any unusual or unique phrase you see in the email and see if others have commented on this particular rumor.

Query	# of Matches
You've heard of a fine public university in the lower left corner of the United States, and you want to know more about it. Try this search: This exact wording or phrase: San Diego State University	Write the number of hits you get below.
Here's how to search for it poorly: All these words: San Diego State University	
Here are some more searches to try: This exact wording or phrase: Bill 602P	
This exact wording or phrase: We know he has weapons of mass destruction	
This exact wording or phrase: demonstrating genuine leadership	
This exact wording or phrase: Jenny kissed me when we met	

Net 3: Trim Back the URL

The next net is not Google specific, though you'll find yourself using it often once you get better at Googling.

You'll find a terrific page nestled deep down inside a folder inside a folder inside a folder. You suspect that there are other pages on the main site that you'd find interesting. How do you find them? Trim the URL step by step.

Sometimes you'll get a notice saying FORBIDDEN! Sometimes you'll get a list of files and directories. Sometimes you'll get a Web page with more links. Each step back tells you more about where the page came from.

This is also a good strategy to try when a page can't be found (i.e., you get a 404 message). Perhaps someone at the site moved the page into a new folder or renamed a folder. Trace your way back to the top and drill down again to see if you can find it.

You found a *Romeo & Juliet* WebQuest that you really like. Are there more like that where this one came from?

Start here:

http://oncampus.richmond.edu/academics/education/projects/ webquests/shakespeare/

Now trim away the last part:

http://oncampus.richmond.edu/academics/education/projects/ webquests/

What do you see?

Trim it again:

http://oncampus.richmond.edu/academics/education/projects/

http://oncampus.richmond.edu/academics/education/

http://oncampus.richmond.edu/academics/

http://oncampus.richmond.edu/

Now try this:

A friend told you of another cool Shakespeare WebQuest and emailed you the URL:

http://www.longwood.k12.ny.us/wmi/wq/collin/index.html

That URL turned out to be wrong, though. Can you find the real URL and see if there are other worthy WebQuests at the same site?

Net 4: Look for Similar Pages

Once you've found something you like on Google, it's very easy (and useful) to find similar pages. How? Below the "Advanced Search" fields that you've been using up until now are another two fields.

This "Page-Specific Search" allows you to find pages that Google has deemed to be similar to or linked to any URL you type in.

How does Google know that two pages are similar? The details of the inner workings of search engines are a trade secret, but it's safe to assume that it's based on similarities in the words and the external links on each page. All that matters is that it works surprisingly well, especially when you're not sure what key words to look for.

Use this tool to find more of a good thing. Use it to find pages that are linked to a page you find useful. Chances are, those pages will be useful to you, too.

And there's always ego surfing: if you've uploaded a page of your own to a public server and it's been there for a while, find out who else is linking to it.

Query	# of Matches
Suppose that you've discovered Tapped In, an online community of educators, and you're wondering what else like that is out there. Google's Page-Specific Search will surface a number of sites that are likely to interest you. Find pages similar to the page: **www.tappedin.org**.	Write the number of hits you get below.
Another way to explore a domain is to find out who else is linked to a page. Who else finds Tapped In useful enough to include it on one of their pages? Find pages that link to the page: **www.tappedin.org**.	
Here's another search to try: Find pages similar to the page: **kids.msfc.nasa.gov**.	
Find pages that link to the page: **kids.msfc.nasa.gov**.	

So, to recap, remembering the word *NETS* will help you remember the four techniques you just experimented with:

Start **N**arrow

Use **E**xact Phrases

Trim the URL

Seek Similar Pages

Keep these four phrases in mind, and you'll be a much better searcher than you were a few minutes ago!

And to add to your bag of tricks, you might also want to check out the Specialized Search Engines section of the WebQuest site (**http://webquest.sdsu.edu/searching/specialized.html**). Or, try out some other Google services and hacks!

Written by Bernie Dodge. Last updated January 22, 2008. There are also Spanish, U.K. (new), and multipage versions.

Be sure to look at the appendix by Bernie Dodge titled "Specialized Search Engines and Directories."

Bernie Dodge, Ph.D., is a professor of educational technology at San Diego State University, where he teaches courses in technology integration and educational game design. He has helped design the staff development program for three Challenge Grants. In 2000, he was named by the editors of *eSchool News* as one of the top 30 educators who have had an impact on technology in the nation's schools. Later that year, *Converge* magazine profiled him among leaders shaping the future of education and technology. Dodge is currently on the Advisory Board for the eMINTS National Center and the Teach the Teachers Consortium. He was named an Apple Distinguished Educator in 2003 and was the recipient of awards from MERLOT in 2004 and 2007. He developed the WebQuest model in 1995 and continues to refine and disseminate it widely through presentations and workshops around the globe and through his website at **http://webquest.org**. To contact Dodge, write him at bdodge@sdsu.edu. (A WebQuest is "an inquiry-oriented activity in which most or all of the information used by learners is drawn from the Web. WebQuests are designed to use learners' time well, to focus on using information rather than looking for it, and to support learners' thinking at the levels of analysis, synthesis, and evaluation.")

Search Strategies Activity Sheet

By Bernie Dodge, Ph.D.

This activity sheet is designed to accompany "Four NETS for Better Searching." Print it out (reduced to fit on one page), record your answers, and think about why the numbers came out that way.

Query	# of Matches	Reasons
WITH ALL: Atlantis continent WITHOUT: shuttle film movie	Example: 417,000	The first shows only what? And excludes what? The second one has more hits because ...
WITH ALL: Atlantis		
WITH ALL: Waterbury WITH AT LEAST ONE: Vermont VT WITHOUT: Connecticut CT		
WITH: Waterbury		
EXACT PHRASE: San Diego State University		The second one has more hits because ...
WITH ALL: San Diego State University		
EXACT PHRASE: Bill 602P		What do these show?
EXACT PHRASE: demonstrating genuine leadership		
EXACT PHRASE: Jenny kissed me when we met		
SIMILAR TO: www.tappedin.org		These are different because ...
LINKED TO: www.tappedin.org		
SIMILAR TO: kids.msfc.nasa.gov		These are different because ...
LINKED IN: kids.msfc.nasa.gov		
Write your question here:		Make up your own search now with different combinations of terms. Write down your search terms and record the number of hits you get.

This page by Bernie Dodge. Last updated January 23, 2007.

Chapter 7

The World of Libraries

When I was a kid, one of the things I looked forward to every summer was the reading contest at the library. You would sign up, check out books, and read. When you finished a book, you would go back to the library, and the librarian, depending on that year's theme, would put a dragon or a clown or a butterfly or a flower on the wall of the children's room of the library. Every time you finished a book, another shape would be added to your area on the wall, and over the summer, you watched it grow. Very satisfying.

I still love books, and prefer them in the form that I can hold in my hands. But I also appreciate the people, places, and things I can access on the Internet, including some materials that are not available at my local library or school media center.

In this chapter, we will look at libraries and librarians with a focus on how librarians and media specialists evaluate information and help teachers and children build critical-thinking skills in terms of selecting and using media.

I interviewed three librarians: a school media specialist, a public librarian, and a librarian at the Library of Congress. Kathy Schrock is the administrator for technology for Nauset Public Schools in Orleans, Massachusetts. She created and still maintains a vast website, Kathy Schrock's Guide for Educators at **http://school.discoveryeducation. com/schrockguide/** with links to many materials for teachers and students on a multitude of subjects.

Gay Ducey is a children's librarian (and nationally recognized storyteller) who runs the children's room at the Rockridge Branch of the Oakland Public Library in Oakland, California.

Leni Donlan, a former teacher, worked at the Library of Congress (LOC) in Washington, D.C., where she served as coordinator of the Learning Page Project: **http://memory.loc.gov/learn**. Unfortunately, Donlan passed away in 2007, but the materials and processes she and her team put in place are still available, along with the new materials that are being added on a regular basis.

I have never met Marsha Ann Tate or Jan Alexander in person, but they have influenced how I look at websites for a number of years. Tate and Alexander are librarians at Wolfgram Memorial Library at Widener University in Chester, Pennsylvania. They are pioneers in looking at the criteria librarians have always applied to evaluating books and helping teachers and students see how those same criteria apply to websites. See Evaluating Web Resources at **http:// www3.widener.edu/Academics/Libraries/Wolfgram_Memorial_ Library/Evaluate_Web_Pages/Checklist_for_an_Information_ Web_Page/5720/** for more information. (See chapter 2 for more information on this topic, as well as a student activity for evaluating Web pages using these criteria.)

Libraries have always been the repository of information within a school or community where students, teachers, and community members can find what they need on every imaginable topic. All of a library's resources have been carefully selected for their value to the school or community. Librarians are trained to evaluate information and make selections based on tried-and-true criteria.

By working closely with our school, the public, and online librarians and libraries, we can further all areas of literacy, help students develop important critical-thinking skills, and encourage lifelong learning and curiosity.

One of the most valuable pieces of information I gained from talking with these librarians is the idea that the same criteria that are used to evaluate books for inclusion in a library apply across all media. While the terms used vary, the five criteria—authority, accuracy, objectivity, currency, coverage—identified by Tate and Alexander seem to cover the field. The three librarians in this chapter approach information sources from different angles, but they still use these criteria for evaluating the sources they provide.

In my interview with Kathy Schrock, I asked her a number of questions about her work, how she views the tremendous amount of information bombarding us these days, and how teachers can help students approach and deal with what they encounter.

Q. As a media specialist, what do you consider the most important skills teachers and students can develop to deal with the overwhelming amount of information available today?

A. First, teachers and students must be able to define their information need by preplanning and identifying what they are actually searching for. Next, they need to be able to search effectively, eliminating unnecessary information as they home in on their stated goal. Examining how others view the information discovered is another skill. Backward searching and citations to good information from trusted experts in the field can go a long way in determining the authority of the creator and the validity of the information. The users then need to be able to critically evaluate the information they find and either utilize it, search yet again, or perhaps even redefine their information need. Finally, teachers and students alike need to recognize [that] intellectual property is not in the public domain and learn to cite all information from any source they use, including interviews, websites, books, magazines, Listservs, videos, television shows, and any other of the myriad of information choices available. Think, plan, search, evaluate, use, credit.

Q. What hints and tips do you have for students to help them evaluate information from different media?

A. Students need to apply a critical eye to all information they find. For example, learning about the techniques of video production can help them understand the editing and cutting that goes on during television interview shows to "sway" the audience with sound bites and cutaways.

Studying the aspects considered in the advertising field (audience, market, etc.) can allow students to understand marketing ploys in print and in the media. Taking a look at websites and news articles that provide two different sides to a topic can prompt students into learning more about a topic in order to dispel the biases inherent in these sites. Looking at "before and after" photographs and practicing with image-editing software can bring home the point to students that even photos can't be trusted in this digital age.

Q. What would help students think more critically about the sites they come across on the Internet?

A. There are two ways to have students understand that information on the Internet needs to be looked at with a critical eye. The first is to show them various bogus sites like Feline Reactions to Bearded Men at **http://www.improbable.com/airchives/classical/cat/cat.html** or Dihydrogen Monoxide FAQ at **http://www.dhmo.org/facts.html** and have them use an evaluation form to look at the various aspects of the site. Although the sites might meet all of the criteria for an "acceptable" site, once they are told the information is totally untrue, they begin to speculate on the merits of validating all information they find on the Internet.

The second method to have students think more critically about sites they come across on the Internet is to teach critical evaluation of websites as a process skill. With repeated practice evaluating all sites they are using for a project by completing a formal critical-evaluation form, students will, after a time, internalize the questions they need to ask themselves when examining information. This internalized skill will be helpful in all areas of their life—from e-purchasing to e-zines to e-research (**http://school.discoveryeducation.com/schrockguide/eval.html**).

Q. What are the most important aspects of information/media literacy?

A. I think the most important aspect of information literacy is the intellectual property issue. With the huge amount of information available, it is possible to "borrow" work from others without ever getting found out. The understanding that free information is at risk if credit to the originator is not given is important for both teachers and students to internalize. Attention to the U.S. Copyright and Fair Use Guidelines drives home the point to the school community that all information is not able to be used for all purposes. In addition, asking for permission to use other's property is now very easy to do with the use of email and should be encouraged for both students and teachers. The peer-to-peer file-sharing debate rages on unchecked, but studying the economic ramifications of illegal distribution of copyrighted materials should become a part of every business and computer class in middle and high school, and the ethics of such actions should be considered as well. The Creative Commons project has also been a great help to students, since permissions for use are specifically outlined based on the licenses the originators have chosen to apply to their work.

Q. What are some specific things teachers and students can do to promote information/media literacy?

A. A key question to ask all the time is, "What did they leave out?" When I was in library school, I was amazed to learn about how much editing can take place for a television show production company to get the exact sound bite, for example. A lot of teachers and students don't realize something has been left out. One way to make sure you are getting good information is to look at other sites, other videos, other materials on the same subject, and compare what you find from multiple sources. Then, you can ask yourself why something in particular didn't show up in one source but can be found in others. Why didn't it show up on a particular site? This gets to the idea of authority: who produced the information, why did they choose to include the material they did, and what are they about?

Image editing is another obvious example. We've all seen pictures in *Star* magazines where heads have been placed on other people's bodies. It's easy to edit images—and it's important to question whether or not you can trust the images you're seeing. The more you look and compare and question, the better you can trust that you know enough about a topic to make a wise decision about the sources you are using.

Another thing I've done is send the questions from Hall Davidson's Copyright Quiz (see pages 115-117) through email to everyone on staff—one question a week. The next week, I will send around another question, along with the answer to the question I sent earlier. This generates a lot of discussion among the whole staff. I include everyone—from custodians to superintendents—and I provide a link directly to our Copyright and Fair Use Guidelines Web page: **http://nausetschools.org/ fairuse.htm**.

Of course, helping students understand they need to ask permission to use materials is very important. It's very important, it's easy to do, and usually people say yes and are pleased to have been asked!

Finally, it all comes down to modeling. Teachers need to understand the importance of all these processes and model them for students. If not, the kids will never get it. Think, plan, search, evaluate, use, credit—that might seem like a lot of steps, but each one is critical. They fit together to complete an important process, and taken together, they make up the skills we all need [in order] to be fully functioning, responsible users and creators of information.

Kathy Schrock can be reached at Kathy@kathyschrock.net.

Gay Ducey and I talked about the role of the public library in helping community members of all ages access information, be fully informed about it, and be able to use it thoughtfully. She reveals a disturbing trend she has seen grow over the years as students continue to be exposed to more and more information.

Q. What processes for selecting resources are available in the library, with an eye toward information literacy? That is, how does a librarian determine what will be in the library collection?

A. Most library systems have a collection development policy or statement that determines what kinds of things to consider when you are getting books and visual materials. Libraries buy good books. When we select materials for the library, we choose them based on reviews from professional journals such as *Library Journal, Horn Book*, and *School Library Journal.* Currency is an important factor—what is new, in demand, or wished for. Coverage refers to that which might fill a hole— that is, broaden or deepen the library's collections. Depending on the size of the library, there may be specialization. For example, in Oakland, California, there are a number of branches that focus on a particular culture—Asian, Latino, African American—as well as on particular collections, such as religious materials or a tool-lending library. The Oakland Main Library houses a nationally recognized collection on the city of Oakland. Librarians locate and catalogue everything about that community. The collection includes magazines, videos, audios, newspapers, etc. There is an emphasis on print materials, although other artifacts are included. There is an obvious mandate for this collection, and such mandates exist in other places as well.

Q. What is the most important role of the public library within a community?

A. The public library provides community members with free access to information. Many people don't think about the community-based service the library offers. It is the most important feature of a public library. At my branch, we have eight PCs; six are available by reservation, and two are kept open on a drop-in basis for patrons to conduct research. We also make movies, CDs, books on tape, and some cassette tapes available for use. (CDs are rare because most have a pedagogical use, and the school rather than the library supplies them.) We also maintain an image collection, a collection of newspapers from many places, a collection of government documents, owners' manuals for cars and tractors, and one of the most important sheet music collections in the area. Through interlibrary loan, we can greatly extend the reach to any library in the world, usually at the cost of 50 cents to the patron. Ephemeral resources include bulletin boards for announcements and places for community materials. Even in today's time of budget restrictions, the collections themselves are quite impressive and serve the needs of the community.

So, the library is not about books particularly, although books still provide the most effective and thorough access to information. First, there is the sensual information. Books are tactile, pleasing to the senses. You can carry them, fan the pages, smell that cottony smell of old books. There is substantial and publicly developed distribution of books into libraries and bookstores; it is easy to order and get books. A great benefit provided by a library is the fact that you are not as constrained to do any kind of shortcutting that you don't want to do when you really want to understand something. While you can pull information off the Internet, it still doesn't give the sense of research. Reading one random article or 'zine doesn't research make.

The public identifies the public library with books, and they should. They often don't understand that is only one way to access information; there are many others.

For example, a California State Library-funded project, the Librarians' Internet Index, provides an extremely important service (**http://www.lii.org**). Veterans of the Internet contribute content to this site that includes a subject index with an annotation for every entry. It may not list all the sites available, but it presents a manageable list of the best sites on a particular topic.

Q. What ideas do you have to help students think critically about what they are reading?

A. What I'd like to see is librarians going into schools or having classes come to them so that librarians could acquaint teachers and students with the idea of critical thinking as it relates to information sources. If we removed this idea from education per se, kids would be more likely to engage. We can promote the acquisition of critical-thinking skills in formalized ways. We have done a bad job as educators by saying, in large part, that is what education is: the acquisition and application of knowledge. It's also very much about the evaluation of information. In my view, we are not raising good citizens, and there's a lot more we could be doing. When you're dealing with helping someone find information, it works best person to person. Kids know what they like. More often, they know what they do not like, but they don't know how to translate that into making good choices about what they want to read.

I think there is a flawed relationship between teachers and librarians. In my experience, there is often a disconnect between what teachers ask kids to do and what they really want them to do. There is very often a confusion about what is expected, so kids are set up to fail in making good use of the public library.

Since the library is the main place to get information you don't have in your house, it's important that teachers and public librarians work together to make library visits meaningful. Kids are less likely to come back to the public library for help if they haven't had a good experience the first time.

The teacher who assigns creative homework (for example, doing a newspaper on the Scopes Monkey Trial, including ads of the period, editorials, letters to the editor, pictures) is doing a good thing, but she should make sure the library knows about the assignment, its intent, and time line. With little direction, no wonder the kid says, "Can't I just get this off the Internet?"

That does not teach children that they have to read to get the information, and you have to read more than you need to in order to find what you need; this is crucial in terms of information. Kids are used to an environment where things are handed to them or they are battered by information. We need to empower kids to evaluate information. Kids can use their libraries to get more of this.

In such a complex society, kids are at an intellectual risk if they get to adolescence without being able to evaluate critical information. We need to build alliances between teachers and librarians.

The job of the public library is a community-based job. Budget cutbacks cut down on the available time we have to go out the front door. But if we can sit down with a teacher for 20 minutes, if we can visit the school two or three times a year, it would make a huge difference in what we can provide students in the library.

Until we find a way to make it real to teachers that we are making common cause in preparing kids for the world, using both these wonderful institutions (libraries and schools), kids aren't going to get better at critical thinking.

Q. What changes have you seen over the years in the students who visit your library?

A. Over the past 20 years, I have really seen the impact of mass media on kids, and I'm very worried: kids are losing language.

My mandate as a children's librarian is to spend as much time as possible with kids—to sit down and talk with kids, not just to answer their questions but to use every contact as an opportunity to forge a little connection. When I sit down and talk with kids today, I notice a very slow and very subtle diminishing ability in expressive language. They don't have the words. What they have is a decreased need for words. They receive information; they do not necessarily solicit it. They sit in front of a TV set, play a video game, watch a video.

There is a diminished amount of contact within homes for conversation, and there is not much incentive to get more.

We communicate through words as a species. If we do not have words, kids can't articulate their experiences and aspirations because they don't have the language to do it. At the same time, we are losing our regional cultures and moving toward a mass culture, so many of the specific words, idioms, and expressions of families and groups have been lost.

We know about shortening attention spans, passive kids, and fat kids, but the most important and critical change is that kids are also losing language, or not gaining it.

It's a fact that he who owns and uses the words has a distinct advantage over he who doesn't.

It's not just how a word is used, but that the word is attached to a culture and history. I find young people who have no idea this is the case. Rarely had they asked themselves about words, or wondered about them. Students need to be encouraged to develop curiosity about words—the defining capacity they have as human beings.

Librarians and teachers must work together to cultivate curiosity and an appetite for learning. If we help children develop lifelong curiosity and interest, if we give them the tools, they'll be fine, and they'll do it all.

Gay Ducey can be reached at mducey@earthlink.net.

Leni Donlan worked with the Learning Page team to develop and maintain the Learning Page on the Library of Congress American Memory site: **http://memory.loc.gov/learn.**

The team continues to do an excellent job of providing students and teachers with access to a wealth of important information. In this interview, we touched on what is available, how it might be used, and particularly, the primary-source material available through the site.

Q. What kinds of media in the Library of Congress are available to students and teachers?

A. Documents, maps, motion pictures, photos and prints, and sound recordings are available. In American Memory, you can search within the specific kinds of media. For example, I'm often looking in the photos and prints section to find illustrations for the Learning Page. From the Learning Page's home page, you can search just our site or all of the Library of Congress websites. You'll find virtually every type of resource.

We also obtain materials through exchange with libraries in this country and abroad: gifts, materials received from local, state, and federal agencies as well as foreign governments, purchase, and copyright deposits. Materials are added to the collections of the library at a rate of 7,000 items per working day. Selection officers review materials and decide which should be kept and added to the permanent collections. Copyright deposits make up the core of the collections, particularly those in the map, music, motion picture, and prints and photographs divisions. Many of the library's holdings come to us and are presented without a great deal of context. Educators may help their students understand the collections by likening them to the "shoebox collections" that we find in our grandparents' attics.

The library offers unparalleled resources for learning about the nation's history but is not the best place to seek information about current affairs and events of the latter part of the twentieth century. Copyright issues prevent sharing of resources from the present and recent past.

Q. What resources from the LOC speak to students becoming critical thinkers about information?

A. All of our resources do because of the shoebox idea. The materials come without a textbook context. They come as they are. They usually raise more questions than they answer. They are the perfect kind of material to use for critical thinking. I highly recommend them!

Q. How can teachers help students look at primary sources critically?

A. We have a number of lessons and activities from Learning Page/ Features & Activities. Two activities I think are particularly useful: one is "Zoom into Maps," which helps students think critically about maps and provides a number of kinds of maps (such as military, environmental, pictorial, local geography maps) to assist in the lesson (**http://memory.loc.gov/learn/ features/maps/index.html**).

"Looking into Holidays Past" uses the seasons to help students learn to analyze primary sources, look at various media types, and learn how to observe critically. The Learning Page lesson plans are chock full of teacher-created and tested lesson plans (**http://memory.loc.gov/learn/features/doc_analysis/index. html**).

Q. What are the copyright rules for information obtained by teachers and students from the LOC?

A. Teachers and students can find most of the information they need from the "How to" section of the Learning Page. Copyright, fair use, citing sources, and other information are available. There is a direct link to the Copyright Office in the copyright page online. Generally, all the resources created for the Learning Page are in the public domain (copyright free) and can be used by educators and students. Of course, citing where information came from is important in student reports and presentations (**http://memory.loc.gov/learn/start/howtos.html**).

We have also developed some collaborative activities in which students can share their findings with the Library of Congress. These activities are based on the idea that we study the past to understand the present and to help shape our future. Two more are coming this year: Interviews with Today's Immigrants, in which students conduct oral history interviews with recent immigrants in their communities to help tell the current story of immigration to the United States. Students can submit their interviews to be published on the Learning Page. The other new collaborative activity will be the America Dreams collaborative project. The initial phase of this project is a WebQuest in which students study the dreams of Americans in past decades, through the "eyes" of politicians, artists, reporters, etc., then create a project showing their understanding of the dream in the era of their research. Next, students will study dreams of the present within their own communities, starting with their families, and, finally, they will contribute to a Wall of Dreams—dreams for their future and the future of our nation (**http://memory.loc.gov/learn/features/index. html#col_activities**).

Q. What are the most important aspects of information/media literacy?

A. I think any use of primary sources demands critical and flexible thinking. And it's a major asset to have such primary sources available. When you're using information of any kind, you have to consider point of view, you have to think about calling upon prior knowledge, you have to think about what you actually see in material, what you know about materials, what you think you know, what hypotheses might tell you and, most importantly, what you want to find out, what it has triggered in your own thinking.

Q. What else is available for teachers at the Learning Page?

A. There is an extensive professional development section. The Library of Congress offers workshops at the Library of Congress, videoconference workshops, and Self-Serve workshops, which can be used independently for local professional development activities at a school or district level. Topics include "Squeezing Documents: Close Reading of Primary Sources" (**http://memory.loc.gov/learn/educators/workshop/squeezing/baover.html**), "Students as Historians: Exercises for the Elementary and Middle School Student" (**http://memory.loc.gov/learn/educators/workshop/sah/hover.html**), search-skills workshops: "Prospecting in American Memory" (**http://memory.loc.gov/learn/educators/workshop/prospecting/prover.html**), and "Searching American Memory" (**http://memory.loc.gov/learn/educators/workshop/search/index.html**).

And there are many, many more workshops. Self-Serve workshops include a "facilitator's guide" and all necessary links and handouts (**http://memory.loc.gov/learn/educators/workshop/ssindex.html**).

The library offers educator institutes, such as one on Lewis and Clark for local educators (or educators able to visit Washington, D.C.). Please visit the Learning Page "News!" section for announcements of such events, as well as new resources available to educators.

Using Primary Sources in the Classroom

The following page from the Library of Congress website suggests a number of activities for using primary sources in your curricula: (**http://memory.loc.gov/learn/lessons/primary.html**).

Suggestions for using primary sources were compiled from the National Digital Library's Educator's Forum held in July 1995 and from the library staff. Educators at the forum, like many throughout the country, know that history comes alive for students who are plugged into primary sources. These suggestions for student activities can help you enhance your social studies curriculum by using authentic artifacts, documents, photographs, and manuscripts from the Library of Congress American Memory Historical Collections and other sources.

I. Source Type: Objects

Sample Primary Sources: artifacts, tools, weapons, inventions, uniforms, fashion

Make a hypothesis about the uses of an unknown object pictured in an old photograph. Use online and library research to support or refute the hypothesis. Make a presentation to the class to "show and tell" the object, hypothesis, search methods, and results.

Use old photographs to study fashion trends. How has fashion changed over time? How did clothing styles reflect people's work and their roles in society? What clothing styles have carried over into present times?

Study old photographs to trace the development of an invention over time (e.g., automobiles, tractors, trains, airplanes, weapons). What do the photographs tell you about the technology, tools, and materials available throughout time? Who used the invention in the past? How is the invention used today?

Sample Primary Sources: tombstones

Write an obituary for a person memorialized on an old tombstone. Use information from the epitaph and research about the era in which the person lived. Research the meaning of stone carvings that appear on the tombstone. Study epidemic illnesses or other circumstances that might explain common causes of death at the time.

II. Source Type: Images

Sample Primary Sources: photographs, film, video

Use a historic photograph or film of a street scene. Give an oral description of the sights, sounds, and smells that surround the scene, presenting evidence from the photograph itself and other sources about the time period. Examine the image to find clues about the economics and commerce of the time.

Select a historical photograph or film frame. Predict what will happen one minute and one hour after the photograph or film was taken. Explain the reasoning behind your predictions.

To encourage a focus on detail, show a photograph or film frame to the classroom for three minutes and then remove it. Have students draw the contents of the image on a piece of paper divided into a grid of nine sections. Repeat this exercise with new images and watch students' abilities to recall detail improve.

Sample Primary Source: fine art

Select a piece of fine art that appeals to your senses. Research the artist, the date of the piece, and the medium. What does information about the artist, the medium, the subject, and the composition tell you about the prevailing attitudes and conditions of the time period? For example, what symbolism is used? How is perspective used? In what roles are people portrayed? What is left out of the composition?

III. Audio

Sample Primary Sources: oral histories, interviews

Research your family history by interviewing relatives. Use letters, audio recordings, and videotape to compile a report on an important time for your family. Make note of differing recollections about the same event.

Work in teams to record interviews of older citizens in the community. Focus on and compile interviews about one aspect of community life, such as work, family, or schools.

Combine class reports with historical images and documents to produce a documentary on the history of your community.

Sample Primary Source: music

Research and study lyrics of popular songs from the periods of World War II, the Korean War, and the Vietnam War. What do the lyrics tell you about public attitudes toward the war? Interview veterans of these wars about their perceptions of the accuracy of the information in the lyrics.

Have students search for events that have inspired lyrics in current popular music. Have students compare present-day events and music to lyrics from the past inspired by historical events. What are the similarities and differences between present-day and historical songs and the events that inspired them?

Sample Primary Source: audio recordings

Introduce an audio recording of a famous political speech. Ask students to think about and write down impressions while they listen to the speech. What is the speaker's key message? What is the speaker's point of view? How does the speaker's oratorical style affect the impact of the message? If the text of the speech is available, have students compare their impressions from hearing the speech to their impressions from reading the speech.

Have students listen to audio recordings from old radio broadcasts.

Compare the language, style of speaking, and content to radio and television programs today. How does the content of the older radio broadcast exemplify the events and prevailing attitudes of the time? How does modern radio and television programming exemplify events and attitudes of the present time?

IV. Statistics

Sample Primary Sources: census data, land surveys, maps, ordinances, blueprints, architectural drawings

Study historical maps of a city, state, or region to find evidence of changes in population, industry, and settlement over time. Use other resources to find and report on causes for the changes you find. Use maps to illustrate your descriptions of these changes.

Choose a famous or historical public building in your area. Research blueprints or architectural drawings of the building. With help from an architect or librarian, compare the plans to the building as it exists today. What changes do you see? Why do you think the changes were made?

V. Text

Sample Primary Source: cookbooks

Research the recipe for a common food (e.g., bread, cake) in cookbooks of different times.

Report on differences in the vocabulary of the cookbooks over time. How have terms for measurement, ingredients, portion size, and accompaniments changed? Prepare the food using recipes from two time periods. Hold a taste test of the end results.

Select a cookbook from another era. Look at the ingredient lists from a large number of recipes. What do the ingredient lists tell you about the types of foods available and the lifestyle of the time?

Sample Primary Source: advertisements

Use old catalog pages to research fashion trends, household articles, cost of living, and lifestyles of a particular period. Use other sources of information to reconstruct a picture of family life at the time. Who did the household purchasing? What were considered necessities of the time? What were considered luxuries? How do the catalog pages highlight attitudes of the time?

Use newspapers over time to analyze advertising. Have students research advertisements for a particular type of product (e.g., clothing, tools, household appliances, automobiles) through history.

What information do the advertisements contain? What claims do they make? Who is the targeted buyer? How has advertising for this product changed over time? What social changes are reflected by changes in advertising for this product?

Sample Primary Sources: journals, letters, diaries

Find firsthand accounts of historical events written by children or young people (e.g., *The Diary of Anne Frank*). Analyze how firsthand accounts give context to historical events. Have students begin keeping their own journals, with an emphasis on including current event topics in their entries.

Select a time period or era. Research and read personal letters that comment on events of the time. Analyze the point of view of the letter writer. Compose a return letter that tells the author how those historical events have affected modern society.

Read a personal diary from a historical period. Analyze the individual's character, motivations, and opinions. Explain how the individual changed over the course of the diary. How might that person react if he or she were dropped into the present time?

Sample Primary Source: documents in the original handwriting or language

Decipher the original text of a famous document (e.g., the

Constitution, the Bill of Rights) by decoding historical lettering, spelling, grammar, and usage. Compare the original writing with printed versions of the document today. What has changed?

To help illustrate the writing process, study draft copies of famous documents. Look at how side notes, additions, and crossed-out words were used to edit the document. Discuss how the changes affected the meaning of the finished work. Have students practice editing their own writing using similar tools.

VI. The Community

Sample Primary Sources: family photographs (e.g., of ancestors and their homes), memorabilia, souvenirs, recipes, ancestors' clothes and papers, oral histories, local historical societies, genealogical information

Make a record of family treasures (e.g., books, tools, musical instruments, tickets, letters, photographs) using photographs, photocopies, drawings, recordings, or videotapes. Put the treasures into the larger historical context of local, state, country, or world events. What was happening in the world when your ancestors were using the family treasures? How did those events affect your family?

Find original letters written by an ancestor. Read the letters and then research the time and events surrounding the letters in other sources. Analyze the opinions and views of the letter writer based on the time and events of the period.

Trace your ancestry to a country or countries of origin. Research the customs, language, dress, food, and cultural traditions of your ancestral country or countries. Prepare a class presentation on your cultural background. Include exhibits and recipes or prepared food from your ancestral country. Describe how your family came to live in your community today.

Prepare a community time capsule with the class. What primary sources will you include to describe your present-day community to future generations? What important information do you wish to convey? Which primary sources will get your message across? When should your time capsule be opened?

Sample Primary Source: physical surroundings

Research the history of famous buildings and popular sites in your community at the local library or historical society. Use disposable cameras to make visual records of these sites in the community as they appear today. Compare your photographs to historical descriptions and older pictures of sites. What changes have occurred? Why?

Trace the ages of buildings in your community. Which is the oldest structure? Which is the newest structure? Research styles of architecture, commonly used building materials, and the roles of buildings through time. How do your community's buildings reflect the evolution of architectural styles and community institutions?

With the help of a local historical society, organize a tour of older homes in your community. Research the ages and historical period of interesting houses you find. Who lived in these homes when they were first built? How do the styles and locations of the homes reflect the roles of the original owners in the community? Research and describe furnishings and decorating styles from the times the homes were built. Do the homes look different today?

Activity: Word Study

Introduction:

The study of the origin of words is fascinating, but few students are exposed to where words come from. In this activity, students will select a number of words to research and then share their discoveries with the class. You will probably want to review the Merriam-Webster Online (**http://www.m-w.com**), Free Dictionary (**http://www.thefreedictionary.com**), and Dictionary.com (**http://www.dictionary.reference.com**) websites before starting this activity. Be aware that some of these sites include ads.

Objectives:

- Students will become etymologists.

- Students will become familiar with tools for word study, including online dictionaries and the *Oxford English Dictionary*.

- Students will begin collecting interesting words and their etymologies and use them in sentences.

Materials:

- computer access, with projection; paper and pencils; standard (paper) dictionary or dictionaries; cards with interesting words on them (you may decide to use spelling words, or go to a site such as Merriam-Webster Online and check out the word lists at Spell It! at **http://www.myspellit.com/**); copies of the Word Card Template and Example (page 172) for each student

Procedure:

1. Ask students what they know about the origin of words. Let them know that words come to English from many sources. Tell them

they will become etymologists—people who find out about where words come from, how their uses have changed over time, and the historical impact the words have had on cultures and societies.

2. Choose a word and discuss its etymology. For example, according to the Merriam-Webster Online Dictionary (**http://www.m-w.com/home.htm**), the word *family* comes from "the Middle English familie, from Latin familia household (including servants as well as kin of the householder), from famulus servant."

3. Explain that students will begin building a collection of words and their origins.

4. Have students pick a word from the word cards you have made and ask them to look up the definition and etymology. They can use your classroom dictionary or dictionaries, or go online to Dictionary.com, the Free Dictionary, Merriam-Webster Online, or even Google (enter the phrase "what is" and the word with no punctuation—e.g., *what is ebullient*—and you will get the standard kind of listing of related sites, but the top entry provides a definition and links to other definition sites).

5. Go to the computer and show students Merriam-Webster Online (**http://www.m-w.com/home.htm**) and the Word of the Day. Click More under the Word of the Day and then the audio symbol to hear the pronunciation of the word. Have one student read the word in a sentence and another read the information about its origin. Start a short discussion about what you have learned. (e.g., Did students know the word already? How about its origin? Were they surprised? What was interesting? What else would they like to know?) Make a word card for this word, and let students know they will be building a file of interesting words. They will locate words (from conversations or speeches, from their spelling words, from their research, from their reading, etc.) that they want to know more about, research the etymology, and write the information on a card, along with the word used in a sentence. They will then add this card to the class file. Occasionally, select a word from the file and challenge students to define the word and/or use it in a sentence.

6. Show students the Spell It! section of this website (**http://www.myspellit.com/**) and encourage them to find and define interesting words from different languages.

7. Tell students that they will be selecting five words, researching them, and making word cards for the class file.

8. Let students know that they can choose their own words or go online and select from words of the day (an archive of words can be found on the Merriam-Webster site, for example).

9. Have students share their most interesting words with the class.

10. Have students add more words to the class word collection on a regular basis.

Reflection:

Helping students become more aware of words—the words they use, where the words come from, multiple meanings of words, etc.—will increase their linguistic intelligence as well as their vocabularies. Being able to apply the exact word to communicate what you mean benefits both speaker and listener or reader. At any time, you can expand the content on the word cards to include part of speech, synonyms, antonyms, or other features.

Word Card Template and Example

Word File Template

Word: _____

_____

Definition: _____

_____

Use in a sentence: _____

_____

Etymology: _____

_____

Source: _____

_____

Example:

Word File Template

Word: <u>mercurial</u>

Definition: <u>quick and changeable in temperament; volatile</u>

Use in a sentence: <u>Her mercurial behavior confused us.</u>

Etymology: <u>Middle English, of the planet Mercury, from Latin *mercurilis*, of the god or planet Mercury, from Mercurius, Mercury</u>

Source: <u>The Free Dictionary http://www.thefreedictionary.com/ mercurial</u>

Activity: Library Linkup

Introduction:

To help students get the most out of their library experiences, bridges need to be built between school facilities and local public libraries. In this activity, teachers and students will begin to learn more about what is available at their schools and within their communities that will support teaching and learning.

Objectives:

- Students will become familiar with school library resources.

- Students will become familiar with the resources of their public library.

- Students will begin to develop a relationship with library staff.

Materials:

- large K-W-L-H chart for brainstorming, paper and pencils, copies of the Library Information Sheet (page 175) for each student

Procedure:

1. Prepare a large K-W-L-H chart on chart paper.

2. Engage students in a discussion about libraries. Ask students what role they think a library plays in a community. Find out how many students have visited the school library and a public library, and how often. Ask them to share some of their experiences.

3. Have students enter ideas into the K-W-L-H chart regarding the resources available at libraries. (Be sure to include primary sources as part of the discussion.)

4. Invite your school librarian/media specialist into class to talk about what's available at school to support reading, research, and

projects. Set up a visit or series of visits to the school library during which the librarian/media specialist can familiarize students with the layout of the library and answer questions about how to locate good information.

5. If there is a public library close enough to the school, arrange for a visit. Make sure a librarian will be available to talk with your class about resources available to students. If appropriate, arrange for students to fill out forms for library cards before the visit so they can check out material while they are there.

6. After the library visits, have students share their thoughts about what is available at both school and community libraries and when they might use each set of collections.

7. Add more to the K-W-L-H chart based on the information students received during their visits. Continue to add to the chart as students use the school and community libraries.

8. Assign a project in which students use the Internet to research local and worldwide libraries. Instruct them to fill out a Library Information Sheet for each library, and collect them in a book for future use. (When assignments for research projects are made, students will have a starting point for their research, both for in-person contacts and online resources.)

Reflection:

Be sure you include your school librarian/media specialist when planning these discussions and visits. You may be surprised by the support your local library can offer you. When the school widens its reach to include community organizations such as the public library, everyone wins. Public librarians can provide a better service to students and teachers, and students continue to develop meaningful patterns for lifelong learning. Include the Internet Public Library (**http://www.ipl.org/**) and the Library of Congress (**http://www.loc. gov/**) in the websites you make available to students.

Library Information Sheet

Name: _____ Date: _____

Fill in the appropriate information for the libraries you visit, whether physically or online. On the Location line, indicate a physical address for local libraries or the URL for online libraries.

1. Library Name: _____

   Location: _____

   Special Features: _____

   Contact Person: _____

2. Library Name: _____

   Location: _____

   Special Features: _____

   Contact Person: _____

3. Library Name: _____

   Location: _____

   Special Features: _____

   Contact Person: _____

Library Information Sheet Sample

Name: <u>Sara Armstrong</u>   Date: <u>12/14/07</u>

Fill in the appropriate information for the libraries you visit, whether physically or online. On the Location line, indicate a physical address for local libraries or the URL for online libraries.

1. Library Name: <u>Oakland Public Library—Rockridge Branch</u>

   Location: <u>5366 College Ave., Oakland, CA 94618</u>

   Special Features: <u>Good children's and teen collections</u>

   Contact Person: <u>Gay Ducey</u>

2. Library Name: <u>Internet Public Library</u>

   Location: **<u>http://www.ipl.org/</u>**

   Special Features: <u>KidSpace, TeenSpace, Presidents of the United States, Native American Authors, and Polar Bear Expedition Digital Collections</u>

   Contact Person: <u>online</u>

3. Library Name: <u>Library of Congress, Kids, Families Section</u>

   Location: **<u>http://www.loc.gov/families/</u>**

   Special Features: <u>America's Library, American Memory, Everyday Mysteries, and Places in the News</u>

   Contact Person: <u>online</u>

Part 3:
GO!–

Harnessing Information

Chapter 8

It's a 2.0 World

With all the advances on the Web, there are many opportunities for students (and teachers!) to become producers rather than simply consumers. Many of the media we have talked about in this book are passive rather than active; however, the intent of this book is to engage students and teachers in regularly questioning and exploring the information we receive from all forms of media. In this chapter, we will look briefly at some of the new technologies that are available that allow us all to do more than simply watch or listen. All of these advances need to be explored and assessed for their educational value and made available to students in ways that make sense.

Early in my teaching career, I had the opportunity to participate in a project mounted by the then Atari Educational Institute. It linked pairs of schools through 300 BAUD modems. My students participated for several years in an interactive book talk with another school 200 miles away. Each week, a group of kids at each school—who had read the same story and generated interesting questions in the Junior Great Books model—came to the computer while an adult at each school typed in a question and then recorded the students' names and their responses to the questions. This was a powerful introduction to the possibility of connecting kids, who then shared their ideas with other kids they ordinarily would not have a chance to meet. I still consider this the most powerful use of the Web—connecting and collaborating. As you will see, with Web 2.0 tools—often called the Read/Write Web—all of us have many chances to participate in what David Warlick calls the "great conversation." That is, we have access to one another globally on a daily basis, and it is important to make our views as educators known in order to contribute to policymaking and legislation that affect our classrooms. Of course, many of the twenty-first century skills we discussed in the first chapter of this book can be addressed by engaging in the conversation and using Web 2.0 tools. Let us also consider what we need to know and do in order to be responsible conversationalists and to help our children be safe, effective contributors as well.

Online Interactions

Netiquette

A number of years ago, when email started becoming popular, people were struck by the way messages could easily be misinterpreted. Since the writer and sender were not face to face, they could not pick up on the cues we send in our body language. Of course, correspondents through "snail mail" already know this, but good letter writers think carefully about what they are writing and use the right words to make sure they are understood. Email is so easy and quick, you can send a message almost without thinking. Also, sarcasm and words that in person could be understood as a joke may come across as hurtful on your computer. Emoticons were developed to try to address just this issue :-). Those little faces made with keyboard characters were meant to take the possible sting out of a message and convey friendliness. Letter combinations that are composed of the initial letters of words in a phrase also grew to provide more personal and quicker communication, such as *lol* for "laughing out loud" when the writer wants to indicate that he or she is amused. The SearchMobileComputing.com site (**http://searchmobilecomputing.techtarget.com/sDefinition/0,,sid40_gci212057,00.html**) will give you more information and more examples of emoticons than you could ever use! The main point of this discussion is to let students know that when they are sending a message to others via email, it may not be received in the exact way they intended. So, taking extra care before hitting "Send" is always a good idea. Reread what you write, change it if you have to, and then send it. And remember, you can never assume that anything you send out on the Internet will remain private.

While instant messenging has been growing in popularity and often takes the place of email, similar concerns about clearly conveying the intent of a message may not be so critical, since the often abbreviated form of instant messages is accepted within the culture of IMers. Perhaps using acronyms for phrases (e.g., bff for *best friends forever*), numbers for words (e.g., 2 equals *to* and 4 equals *for*), and other such language adaptations help define members of IM communities (e.g., friends, work associates, families) and confirm their identity and membership in the group. However, it seems appropriate to call attention to the communication model by coding/decoding such messages, at least for the sake of classroom discussions and clear communication.

Cyber Safety

With all the Internet access students have, issues of safety in the online world have emerged. Some children have been victimized by online predators; however, according to Larry Magid and Anne Collier in their book *MySpace Unraveled: A Parent's Guide to Teen Social Networking*, the number is much smaller than the media seems to indicate. Regardless of the number of victims, there are concerns that must be addressed and ways that all of us can stay safe online. For example, instruct students never to provide personal information. This includes full name, address, phone number, school name, favorite places to shop or hang out—any information that would allow a student to be identified and physically contacted or located. See **http://www.ctap4.org/cybersafety/pi.htm** for more information about protecting personal information and **http://www.ctap4.org/cybersafety/cp.htm** for more about cyber predators and how to stay cyber safe for teachers, parents, and students.

Cyber Bullying

Cyber bullying—the online version of bullying—refers to using online tools to harass, tease, or put down kids for any sensitive topic—looks, behaviors, choice of friends, etc. Unfortunately, cyber bullies are most often other kids. The best way to prevent cyber bullying is to help students understand how hurtful and damaging this kind of behavior can be—in person and online. In a recent issue of *Greater Good* (**http://www.greatergoodmag.org**), in an article titled "Playground Heroes: Who Can Stop Bullying?" authors Ken Rigby, Ph.D., and Bruce Johnson, Ph.D., say, "Once children know how their peers feel about bullying, there is a good chance that some of them will be influenced by what they have learned." There are many online resources for teachers, parents, and students to support conversations, role-playing scenarios, and other awareness-building activities. See **http://www.ctap4.org/cybersafety/cb.htm** for further information and ideas.

Focus on Writing

Blogs

Weblogs, or blogs, are a way for anyone online to share his or her ideas on any topic at any time. This, of course, means there is good news and bad news. The good news is that all can make their views known, while the bad news is that since the views are personal, they may be offensive, unfounded, or just plain dull. I believe, however, that the good news outweighs the bad. There are some wonderful blogs that address educational issues. Take a look at David Warlick's blog "2¢ Worth: Teaching & Learning in the new education landscape" (**http://davidwarlick.com/2cents/**), Will Richardson's blog "Weblogg-ed: Learning with the Read/Write Web" at **http://weblogg-ed.com/about/**, and Kathy Schrock's "Kaffeeklatsch" at **http://kathyschrock.net/blog/**. If those are not enough, there are a number of Web users online who have started to catalog blogs and provide links. Kathy Schrock's Educational Technology Blog Listing is a good place to start (**http://kathyschrock.net/edtechblogs.htm**).

Will Richardson is a pioneer in the area of using blogs in the classroom. At his site, you can learn about the first blog he and his students set up, which was about the book *The Secret Life of Bee*s and how they got into conversation with its author, Sue Monk Kidd. You can also find a link to Blogs on Educational Blogging (**http://supportblogging.com/Links+to+School+Bloggers**) and much more. If you decide that a blog would work well in your classroom, you can set up blogs free through Blogger.com (**http://www.blogger.com/start**).

Along with the ease of setting up a blog and sharing ideas online is the obvious fact that blogging is a written exercise. While we know that students care more about a piece of writing they post online that can be seen by the global community than one written for a teacher alone, having students blog reaps the same benefits as other written assignments. As David Warlick suggests in his book *Classroom Blogging: A Teacher's Guide to Blogs, Wikis, & Other Tools That Are Shaping a New Information Landscape*, blogs offer a way for each of us to share our views and participate with others in global conversations.

Perhaps there are three phases to your involvement with blogs. The first phase might be called "lurking," which means that you can check in on particular blogs, or even subscribe to them, but not comment yourself. Through reading what was posted, as well as the comments made by others, you can access good information and monitor the content and tone to see if this is a blog you want to continue to read. If you decide this is the case, it is very easy to set up a free account on Bloglines (**http://www.bloglines.com**), for example, where you identify blogs you want to track. As you check your Bloglines page, you will see how many new postings have been made to the blogs you have chosen, and you can link directly to those blogs to catch up on what you have missed.

The second phase in blogging involves writing comments in response to what you have read. The power of blogging lies not only in the idea that others read and agree with the writer's thoughts but also that a conversation is taking place, and the writer gains from readers' responses as well. It's very easy to make comments. Usually, there is a button that says "Comments" that, when clicked, will give you a space to write your response, after which you click Submit for posting. Your comment will then be listed among the others, and you may find others commenting on your comment! Thus, the conversation continues.

Finally, the third phase is setting up your own blog, which is very simple to do at sites such as Blogger.com (**http://www.blogger.com**) or Edublogs (**http://www.edublogs.com**), which is dedicated to teachers and students. Just as we discussed earlier, when you set up and write your blog, you are sharing your thoughts with the global community. We sometimes caution students to think about their parents' reaction to an email they are thinking of sending out—and if they would be offended, it might not be a good idea to send it. The same is true with blogging; what you and your students write will be around forever, so it is important to make sure spelling and punctuation are accurate, and the message is clear, responsible, and thoughtfully crafted. Logistically, it is often a good practice to craft a blog message in a word-processing program, which gives you time and space to request feedback, reread and edit it, and then copy and paste it into the designated space for your blog. While some discussions can become heated when we speak face to face, the words eventually fade away, but if we say the same things online, they remain there for everyone to see.

That being said, it is important to consider blogging as a professional, as well as including this Web 2.0 tool in our classrooms. Take a look at Barbara Ganley's blogs at Mt. Middlebury College, Middlebury, Vermont (**http://mt.middlebury.edu/middblogs/ ganley/bgblogging/**). While Ganley is a college professor, her ideas for blogs can cross grade levels and curriculum areas. Since students become better at writing by doing exactly that, having a worldwide forum in which to write and receive responses stimulates thinking and creativity—and improves writing. Whether you are asking students to participate in a blog that involves writing 100 words on a topic, sharing it, and then commenting on other students' posts on the same topic, or if you are having students share their research on a social studies topic, their deconstruction of a math or science theorem, or their reflections on any learning they have done, blogs are another way for students to share their understanding of concepts and comment on the expressions of understanding of their peers. Will Richardson, a pioneer in classroom blogging, says, "The possibilities really are endless. But by their very structure, blogs facilitate what I think is a new form of genre that could be called 'connective writing,' a form that forces those who do it to read carefully and critically, that demands clarity and cogency in its construction, that is done for a wide audience, and that links to the sources of the ideas expressed" (Richardson, 2006, p. 29).

Just as we earlier discussed the importance of thoughtful evaluation of website information, we must help our students understand that the content of blogs is often personal opinion and must be verified if it is to be cited in research. And we must give them the opportunity to experiment with blogs and other Web 2.0 tools so that they can discover the benefits and drawbacks on their own.

Visit these sites for more curriculum ideas and information about the use of blogs in the classroom:

Will Richardson's famous *The Secret Life of Bees* blog (2002) at **http://weblogs.hcrhs.k12.nj.us/bees/**

Will Richardson's main blogging page, weblogg-ed at **http://weblogg-ed.com/**

Anne Davis, an information systems training specialist in the College of Education at Georgia State University, is another pioneer. See her main page, EduBlog Insights, at **http://anne.teachesme.com/**.

Anne Davis's Blogical Minds (fifth graders using blogs at **http://itc.blogs.com/minds/**).

When you are ready to create your own classroom blog, visit David Warlick's Class Blogmeister site for easy, free access at **http://classblogmeister.com/**.

Wikis

What is a wiki, and what is the difference between blogs and wikis? A wiki is an online area where a group of people can work collaboratively by creating postings and then editing them. Wikis are very good for work on a project that will end in a product of some kind: for example, a paper and presentation or a report. They differ from blogs in that there is more than one author, and the visible version changes with editing, although there is a record of the different versions so everyone can see the changes and who made them.

Perhaps the most famous wiki is Wikipedia (**http://www.wikipedia.org**). Wikipedia is the fastest-growing online encyclopedia enhanced and maintained mainly by volunteers. While some educators cast aspersions on the efficacy of entries in Wikipedia, more Nobel Prize winners have contributed to Wikipedia than any print encyclopedia. The power of Wikipedia is the ease with which information can be posted and updated. In fact, while I suggest that students confirm their findings on Wikipedia with other sources, the information there is often more reliable than most print resources because of its immediacy. According to Don Tapscott and Anthony D. Williams in their book *Wikinomics: How Mass Collaboration Changes Everything*, "an average of nearly two thousand new English-language articles are posted every day on every imaginable subject." The authors go on to say that because the articles are vetted by volunteers passionate about the subjects, accuracy emerges fairly quickly. An intriguing feature of this site is the ability to track the changes and see the discussions around changes that were made.

Just as with blogs, there can be three stages of engagement in a wiki for classroom use. First comes lurking. Check out any number of wikis, or articles in Wikipedia, and track the changes.

Next comes participation. Add your own edits to Wikipedia articles or other wiki projects to which you are invited.

Finally, create your own wiki. Perhaps you want to work with a colleague on a conference presentation, an article for a journal, or developing a collaborative lesson. By using a wiki, all collaborators see the same iterations of documents at the same time and can edit at any time, leaving a path of changes that others can follow.

When you are ready to set up a wiki, you can easily do so at no charge at **http://www.wikispaces.com**. You will even find a blog there about wikis! The wikispaces developers have also created an area devoted to K–12 education, where you can quickly set up wikis for your classes. See **http://www.wikispaces.com/site/for/teachers** to sign up.

Ideas for classroom use include any collaborative project where students will be planning together, producing a multifaceted product, or building information over time. Will Richardson comments, "The collaborative environment that wikis facilitate can teach students much about how to work with others, how to create community, and how to operate in a world where the creation of knowledge and information is more and more becoming a group effort" (Richardson, 2006, p. 74).

Podcasts

Starting with iPods, the idea of recording audio files and sharing them online has grown into huge collections of audio and now video files on many, many websites. Educators are using podcasts to share student work as well as their own assignments for students who may have missed a class. Creating audio files is very simple. All you need is a way to record digital audio—your computer or a device such as an iPod. Free open-source software called Audacity (**http://audacity. sourceforge.net**) allows for quick and easy audio editing. You can then upload your class podcasts to your school or class Web page for other students, parents, or the world to hear.

Check out the Education Podcast Network (**http://www.epnweb. org/**) for many classroom and professional examples of podcasts. Anything that benefits from being heard can be included in a podcast—a lesson, an interview, directions to a field trip. The possibilities are endless!

Other Social-Networking Tools

The idea that students can be in touch with each other nearly all the time through instant messaging or sites such as MySpace (**http:// www.myspace.com**) or Facebook (**http://www.facebook.com**) supports the current interest in collaboration and sharing. While these twenty-first-century skills become more valuable in school and work, students have already gravitated to such sites and spend a lot of time sharing there. Our job is to help them do so rationally and safely. You may want to create a presence for yourself on Facebook, which is becoming more and more popular with educators, so that you can learn about the interactions, experience being part of an online community, and even participate in discussions with colleagues.

A wonderful example of the positive good and power of social networking sites can be seen at TakingITGlobal—a site where students from around the world exchange ideas and make plans to take action for the good of the planet and its people (**http://www. takingitglobal.org**).

Discussing social-networking tools brings us full circle to considering safety and responsible behavior on the Web. Because we know children can spend an inordinate amount of time on social-networking sites, we need to make sure they understand the ramifications of what they say, the pictures they post, and how they treat others there. It is imperative for students to realize that bits of personal information can be put together to identify who they are and where they can be found. And students must understand the consequences of posting comments about others. Just as the person in the old story learned that trying to take back hurtful words is like attempting to collect feathers in the wind, words on the Web cannot be retrieved and can do permanent, harmful damage. Web 2.0 tools present amazing opportunities for students and teachers to participate in what David Warlick refers to as the "great conversation." They also carry a responsibility for thoughtful and ethical behavior.

As educators, we are being presented with opportunities to learn more about what engages students and to incorporate these tools and practices into the classroom when they make sense. The California Library Association, for example, piloted a free online class that provides instruction for participants in twenty-first-century tools. Recently, two versions were developed—one for classroom teachers and the other for library/media specialists. Visit **http://schoolibrary.org/res/library_2_ 0.htm** to get more information and to sign up for either course.

This is an exciting time to be an educator. With regard to collaboration, creative technology tools, and worldwide interaction, there are more opportunities for learning—and teaching—than ever before.

Activity: Web 2.0 Tools

Introduction:

It's a whole new world in terms of the technology tools that are available to us—and that students feel comfortable using. It is essential that we, as educators, explore what's available and bring what makes sense into our classrooms.

Objectives:

- Educators will explore Web 2.0 tools.
- Educators will engage in conversations with peers about Web 2.0 tools.
- Educators will begin to incorporate Web 2.0 tools into the classroom.

Materials:

- Internet access

Procedure:

1. Go online to the California School Library Association website and participate in the CSLA 2.0 School Library Learning 2.0 online tutorial (**http://schoolibrary.org/res/library_2_0.htm**). Through this activity, you will become familiar with a range of Web 2.0 tools and can think about how they might (or might not) be applied in the classroom.

2. Look at some blogs that discuss using Web 2.0 tools in school:

   David Warlick's blog—"2¢ Worth: Teaching and Learning in the new education landscape" at **http://davidwarlick.com/2cents/**

   Will Richardson's blog—"Weblogg-ed: Learning with the Read/Write Web" at **http://www.weblogg-ed.com**

Kathy Schrock's "Kaffeeklatsch" at **http://kathyschrock.net/blog/**

Kathy Schrock's Educational Technology Blog Listing at **http://kathyschrock.net/edtechblogs.htm.**

3. Interview students of different ages to learn which Web 2.0 tools they are using, for what purpose, and what they think of them. You might also ask them how they think their favorite tools might be used at school.

4. Encourage colleagues to take the CSLA course and talk with their students.

5. Meet as a faculty and share ideas about how Web 2.0 tools might be used at your school.

Reflection:

Engaging students in conversation about effective technology tools for education may reveal some intriguing ideas that will benefit the entire teaching and learning enterprise.

Chapter 9

Developing and Evaluating Multimedia Projects

The purpose of all the chapters in this book comes together in this chapter. Using what we learned about topics covered in previopus chapters, this chapter lists some online multimedia opportunities—many in the form of contests—available to students and takes a look at evaluating projects from a holistic viewpoint.

Perhaps you have decided that having students present knowledge using a variety of media will satisfy a number of requirements, including meeting curriculum, district, state, and ISTE standards; addressing multiple intelligences; engaging students in collaborative work; and asking students to approach a problem from a number of aspects. Because contest designers have often thought carefully about the products they are looking for from a variety of educational perspectives, having students create websites or other multimedia projects often helps them focus on the dimension of effective communication in their work. Students who are producing for an audience larger than the teacher and their peers often respond to the heightened challenge and work harder and longer.

Although the North Central Regional Technology in Education Consortium is no longer in operation, you can still find their very useful Learning with Technology Profile Tool, which can be used to "compare your current instructional practices with a set of indicators for engaged learning and high-performance technology" (**http://www. ncrtec.org/capacity/profile/profwww.htm**). There are a number of categories under two headings: Indicators of Engaged Learning and Indicators of High-Performance Technology. Indicators of engaged learning include instructional models, learning context, student roles, and teacher roles, among others. Indicators of high-performance technology include access, operability, organization, and ease of use.

The profile is intended as a starting point for discussions among staff (and, hopefully, students) on topics regarding how learning best takes place in schools, how students can be included more in making decisions about their own learning, and how to best use technology tools in engaging students in curriculum areas.

At the highest levels of engagement, according to the profile, students have opportunities to "pose questions, initiate projects, and explore issues linked to the curriculum, often with little prior background knowledge." Additionally, they have time to explore "uncharted territory" (e.g., the Internet), and serve as "cognitive apprentices" by "observ[ing], apply[ing], and refin[ing] through practice the thinking processes used by practitioners in specific content areas. They receive ongoing feedback on many aspects of a complex problem or skill."

Also, students "have frequent opportunities to share and discuss what they have learned with others, e.g., jigsawing, reciprocal teaching, demonstrations, and presentations within and outside their classroom," and "students are often involved in instructional activities in which they create novel products and ideas to represent their learning."

Project Design

Well-designed projects in project-based learning meet many needs, including the goal of educators to help students think critically about what they are learning, apply their thinking to the world outside school, and communicate clearly to an authentic audience (e.g., parents, community members, and the world via the Internet). The creation of a good question forms the basis of a successful project and provides a deep and meaningful learning experience for students.

There are a number of people, organizations, and resource materials that focus on project-based learning and provide examples. I will mention three here—Sylvia Chard, the George Lucas Educational Foundation, and the Buck Institute for Education. A number of other examples can be found in the Resources section of this book.

In her pioneering work on project-based learning, Sylvia Chard, Ph.D., professor emerita of the Child Study Centre and professor of early childhood education at the University of Alberta, Edmonton, Canada, has looked long and carefully at the "project approach" and how it benefits student learning. She defines a project as "an in-depth investigation of a real-world problem worthy of children's attention and effort."

At the website (**http://www.project-approach.com/definition. htm**), you will find research on project-based learning, examples, and teaching strategies. Chard divides a project into three phases. In Phase 1, students and teachers decide on a topic, share their previous knowledge of the topic, and develop questions for research. Chard calls Phase 2 "fieldwork." All research, any virtual or actual field trips, compilation of materials, and development of the presentation take place in preparation for Phase 3, when the culminating event allows students to share what they have learned.

Filmmaker George Lucas came to appreciate engaged learning when he went to film school and was allowed to work at what he loved. The foundation he created identifies schools across the country that provide meaningful school experiences for students, such as those that have delved deeply into project-based learning. At the foundation's website (**http://www.edutopia.org**), visitors are encouraged to read stories and view film segments of exemplary practices.

Examples of projects and how teachers across the country have implemented project-based learning can be found in stories and film segments at the George Lucas Educational Foundation website. These examples include Eeva Reeder's high school geometry class in Washington presenting its school designs to a pair of local architects (see "Geometry in the Real World: Students as Architects"); students at Newsome Park Elementary School in Virginia researching cystic fibrosis because one of their classmates suffers from it (see "More

Fun Than a Barrel of…Worms?!"); students at Ben Franklin Middle School in New Jersey putting on their daily TV show (see "We're Here to Raise Kids: Character Development Is Key"); and a student from West Hawaii Explorations Academy presenting her findings on restoring brackish ancient ponds to graduate students at the University of Hawaii ("Classrooms Without Boundaries: Taking Education Outside in Hawaii"). You may want to take a look at the Project-Based Learning Teaching Module for more information and ideas (**http://www.edutopia.org/teaching-module-pbl**).

The Buck Institute for Education (**http://www.bie.org/index. php/site/PBL/overview_pbl/**) promotes the thoughtful use of project-based learning in middle and high schools. Their Project Based Learning Handbook (**http://www.bie.org/index.php/site/PBL/pbl_handbook/**) goes in depth regarding the definition of *project-based learning*, creating good questions, planning a project, and developing meaningful evaluation. The institute has developed two extensive projects for high-school students: Problem Based Economics (**http://www.bie.org/index.php/site/PBE/pbe_overview/**) and Problem Based Government (**http://www.bie.org/index.php/site/PBG/pbg_overview/**).

A number of curriculum-based contests provide already-prepared opportunities for students to participate in projects. Even if having students submit contest entries doesn't sound appealing, you may want to look at these sites for good examples of student work and ideas for projects:

The MY HERO Project

http://www.myhero.com

The MY HERO Project celebrates heroes in text, short films, and art. Students and adults from around the world contribute stories, films, and artwork. A short-film contest is held every year, and filmmakers of all ages and experience levels compete with their peers.

International Schools CyberFair 2008

http://www.globalschoolnet.org/gsncf//index.cfm

This year's theme, Learn and Unite, challenges students to develop Web pages that provide local, specific information. Included in the process is a requirement to fill out a detailed rubric on other student entries.

Island Movie

http://islandmovie.k12.hi.us/

The Island Movie contest, along with its sister event in Alaska—iDidaMovie—asks K–12 students to create short digital movies in one of three categories: "Teach Me Something," "Tell Me a Story," or "Environmental Concerns and Social Issues." The contest is currently open to students in Hawaii public schools.

California Student Media Project

http://www.mediafestival.org

Billed as "the nation's oldest student media festival" and having just entered its 42nd year, this contest is open to schools in California, and "celebrates converging technologies with media and multimedia projects produced by students and teachers."

National Student Television Awards

http://www.nationalstudent.tv/

Sponsored by the National Television Academy, the National Student Television Award of Excellence honors student work in broadcast journalism. As stated in its introduction, the award "is intended to be an incentive for the pursuit of excellence in television journalism and to focus public attention on outstanding achievements in television by high school students."

ThinkQuest

http://www.thinkquest.org/library.html

Now sponsored by the Oracle Education Foundation, the ThinkQuest competition "offers a unique project-based learning experience to students and teachers across the globe." Designed for students ages 13–19, collaboration among teammates from different parts of the world is a hallmark of this contest. Teams develop Web pages on topics within curriculum areas that will teach peers about the topic.

Participation in any of these projects can fulfill the definition of project-based learning. The final product in these cases is often a short film, a website, a story, or a piece of artwork. Each of these presentations provides an opportunity for students to share their work with a wide audience—globally, in the case of materials shared on websites.

Another kind of culminating event for projects is the presentation of results to an interested group. For example, if students explored the water quality of a local stream, they may present their findings to the city council or a local water or environmental group. To prepare for their presentation, a graphic organizer may provide the clearest outline of necessary steps.

Introduce the topic: use pictures of the stream.	Show data in chart form, explaining the findings.	Discuss implications (alter picture of stream showing results if no steps are taken).
Enlist the audience in brainstorming specific action steps; use Inspiration® for recording.	Have the audience prioritize their ideas.	Set dates for action; get agreement for the next step: publish the project online.

Using even a simple diagram such as this, students can plan their presentation, listing what will be needed for each area, locating images, creating charts or other pictures, or developing a script or voice-over for their digital story or movie. Collaborative groups can divide up the work and keep track of what has been completed and what needs to be done.

Project Assessment

Vital to the success of project-based learning is meaningful assessment. Each of the contests mentioned includes a judging phase based on criteria outlined for the contest. The International Schools CyberFair Contest, for example, requires students to judge other submissions as part of their participation in the contest. A comprehensive online rubric (**http://www.globalschoolnet.org/gsncf/rubric//evalrubric.cfm**) guides students and other judges through the criteria for assessing a website.

Other websites provide examples of rubrics, as well as opportunities for teachers and students to build their own rubrics using templates:

- Rubistar (**http://rubistar.4teachers.org/index.php**)

- PBL Checklists (**http://pblchecklist.4teachers.org/checklist.shtml**)

- Rubric Machine (**http://landmark-project.com/rubric_builder/index.php**)

- Rubric Studio and Rubric Gallery (**http://www.rcampus.com/rubricshellc.cfm?mode=gallery&sms=home&srcgoogle&gclid=CJy53ezf4JACFSosagodZBYjXQ**)

These sites might best be used to help students develop rubrics for their own work, using the samples provided, and then moving to original rubrics that clearly state the particular expectations for a project. When students participate in the planning of their projects and the development of the rubrics by which they will be assessed, they are more likely to participate in their project more fully, as well as better understand the requirements of their work.

Quite a bit of research has been done on rubrics and how to write them. Carefully designed rubrics serve as valuable learning tools for students and for teachers as they continue to refine their curricula. Hints to writing good rubrics include clearly stating the goal or intent of the work, developing a good description of exemplary work, and then listing three to four other levels of work one might expect to see. For example, the product of a project may be defined as a presentation to a community group that details findings concerning the water quality of a local stream. Categories within the rubric might assess the quality and completeness of the data collected, the depth of collaboration among group members, the quality and clarity of the presentation, and the thoughtfulness of the proposed action steps. If we take one of these categories—data collection, for example—the four levels might list exemplary research techniques and data analysis for the top level and then detail three lower levels, with the lowest including no data collection or a flawed analysis.

Criteria	Exemplary	Very Good	Average	Flawed
Project quality				
Complete data	Data collection exceeded expectations and included information that allowed for clear conclusions.	Data collection met expectations and included information that allowed for clear conclusions.	Data collection was good but did not include enough information to support clear conclusions.	Data collection was poor and did not include enough information to support clear conclusions.
Collaboration				
Presentation quality				
Presentation clarity				

While rubrics can have almost any number of levels, many rubric designers agree that an even number of levels is better than an odd number because it is a human tendency to lean toward the middle level; whereas, an even number of levels encourages more thoughtful decision making. Also, the terms that head the levels can vary a great deal. Perhaps one helpful way to think about them is this: the top level is a resounding "yes!" The student did a great job, understood the challenge, went the extra yard, etc. The next level is "yes, but," meaning the student did a good job, but there was more that could have been done to really solidify the learning. The next level is "no, but," which indicates that the student certainly did better than the student who missed the point or did not do very much work. Finally, the lowest level is "no"—either no work or not enough was done, or the student did not understand the implications of the work and could not communicate his or her learning. You can develop the labels and content of these levels with your students to make the whole endeavor more meaningful to both them and you.

The most important thing when it comes to building rubrics is being clear at each stage. One common mistake is to try to put too much into a single criterion. For example, if you are spelling out the characteristics of a good oral presentation, you will want to separate out aspects such as clear speaking voice and good eye contact. If you put both of them into the same criterion, it will be difficult to score if the student uses a clear speaking voice but has little eye contact, or vice versa.

As you think about helping students develop their guiding questions for their projects, look at the rubric David Thornburg, Ph.D., developed for evaluating questions, which can be found at the end of his Inquiry paper in the Resources section of this book. This rubric will not only guide you and your students in creating a meaningful rubric for whatever projects they propose but will also help you both when considering and evaluating good questions for your projects.

Activity: Developing a Project-Based Learning Project

Introduction:

In this culminating activity, help students bring together everything they have learned as they work through a project, including formulating penetrating questions, laying out the project or parts of the project using graphic organizers, searching the Internet, locating sources at their public library, citing sources, checking copyright rules, evaluating information sources, and using a variety of sources (e.g., the Internet, books, magazines, interviewing people). You will want to decide on a time frame for the project, with benchmarks for project progress. Start with a small project, since larger projects are quite complex and usually take more time and effort than you initially expect. Perhaps there is an area of study in your social studies or language arts curriculum that lends itself to a student-generated project, offering some choice for students while still meeting standards.

Objectives:

- Students will develop a project.
- Students will use a variety of media, resources, research techniques, and strategies.

Materials:

- graphic-organizer software such as *Inspiration*® or paper and pencil, Internet access, copies of the Project-Based Learning Activity Sheet (page 204) for each student

Procedure:

1. Let students know they will all be starting a major project that will bring together a number of strategies, evaluation skills, questioning techniques, and other information-literacy skills they

have learned.

2. Remind students of the work they have done with developing good questions. Suggest that this project will be on a topic of their choosing (or from a more specific topic or list you have created), and the first step will be to develop a K-W-L-H graphic organizer and to fill in a Question Activity Sheet (see page 89).

3. Hold a class meeting to discuss the project plans. Divide the class into groups of three to four students, and have students present their plans to the members of their group, recording feedback. Suggest that each group select one of the projects to undertake.

4. Remind students of the variety of resources available, including their local library, local experts, online resources, etc.

5. Make sure students are including evaluations of the websites they are using (see the Five Criteria Activity Sheet on page 65). Remind students to cite all sources. (You may want them to use the Son of Citation Machine at **http://citationmachine.net/?resize=1**.)

6. Periodically, have students present their plans to their peers for feedback.

7. When the projects are complete, have students present them to their peers, community members, experts, or other students. Perhaps you will want to post the completed projects on the Web.

Reflection:

As part of the learning process for this activity, ask students to reflect on their work and what they will do differently for the next project. You will probably want to do the same—reflecting on what worked, what did not work so well, what you will do differently next time, how much time you will allow, whom you might involve in the project, etc.

Project-Based Learning Activity Sheet

Name: _____ Date: _____

Fill in the information as you develop it.

1. Team members: _____

2. Project title: _____

3. Essential question: _____

4. List possible research sources. Be as specific as possible. _____
   _____

5. What is the first thing you will do to begin work on the project?
   _____

6. What will each team member be responsible for? _____
   _____

7. Design a rubric for the project.

Criteria	Level 1:	Level 2:	Level 3:	Level 4:	Points

Activity: Creating a Project-Based Learning Rubric

Introduction:

Meaningful evaluation of projects includes performance-based assessment. This means that simply assigning a grade or administering a standardized test is not the best way to assess the learning that has taken place. Developing rubrics with students empowers them by encouraging them to define quality work and know what is expected of them. And while it may be too early to develop a rubric for the specific project each student team will pursue, talking about rubrics and developing a template at this point are helpful in guiding thinking as students begin their work.

Objectives:

- Students will develop a rubric template.

- Students will eventually apply the rubric to a project.

Materials:

- graphic-organizer software such as *Inspiration*® or paper and pencil, Internet access, copies of Evaluation Rubric Activity Sheet (page 207) for each student

Procedure:

1. Discuss with students the idea of a four-level rubric, explaining that having an even number of choices helps evaluators (including the students themselves) think about the quality of work.

2. Brainstorm ideas for the names of the four levels (e.g., Yes; Yes, But; No, But; No; or Exemplary, Advanced, Average, Not Acceptable; or Accomplished, Competent, Developing, Beginning; or Lion, Wolf, Raccoon, Mouse; or Eagle, Condor, Owl, Robin; or 4 points, 3 points, 2 points, 1 point). The point is that the levels can be named anything as long as they are well defined. You can

come to agreement as a class or allow each team to name their own levels. For the sake of this activity, reach some agreement on the labels that will be used.

3. The next step is to consider the categories that will be rated. Again, without knowing what the specific projects will be, this is more difficult than if the project topics were known. However, there are some things you know already: you are probably expecting research (the number of sources explored might be a category), high-quality content, clear presentation, good collaboration, creative materials, etc. Solicit categories from the students and agree on which four you will work on together.

4. Have the whole class work on one criterion together before having students work individually or in groups to fill in the rest. Start with a description of the highest level, then the lowest, and then fill in the other two. Hand out the Evaluation Rubric Activity Sheet. Have students work in groups or individually to come up with the four levels for a particular criterion, and then have them share their ideas with the whole class. Decide whether you will be assigning points to the levels. If not, the points column on the right side of the table can be ignored.

5. Continue to talk about matrices, performance evaluation, authentic assessment, and the development of rubrics in the benchmarks expected as each project progresses.

Reflection:

Developing rubrics to guide student work is a powerful way to engage students in thinking critically about what they are producing. Usually, when students have participated in developing rubrics, or at least understand them very specifically before they start work, they are able to understand how well they have done and the areas in which they can improve with the next project.

Evaluation Rubric Activity Sheet

Name: _____ Date: _____

1. Decide on the names of the four levels you will include in your rubric.
2. In the left column, enter the criteria your class identified.
3. Write the description for the highest level of the criterion (or criteria) you were asked to define.
4. Write the description for the lowest level of the criterion or criteria.
5. Fill in the middle descriptions.

Criteria	Level 1:	Level 2:	Level 3:	Level 4:	Points

Evaluation Rubric Activity Sheet Sample

Name: <u>Sara Armstrong</u> Date: <u>12/23/07</u>

1. Decide on the names of the four levels you will include in your rubric.
2. In the left column, enter the criteria your class identified.
3. Write the description for the highest level of the criterion (or criteria) you were asked to define.
4. Write the description for the lowest level of the criterion or criteria.
5. Fill in the middle descriptions.

Criteria	Level 1: Exemplary	Level 2: Advanced	Level 3: Average	Level 4: Not Acceptable	Points
Research	Research for the project was thorough, multiple sources were used, and all sources were cited.	Research for the project used a number of sources, and all sources were cited.	Research for the project used one or two sources, and they were cited.	Sources were not cited.	
Content	The content created reflected critical thinking and included new ideas based on the research.	The content created reflected good thinking about the research.	The content created begins to get at new ideas based on the research.	The content was little more than a reiteration of the sources.	
Presentation	The presentation was well planned and well executed.	The presentation was well planned, but there were some glitches.	The presentation lacked some planning, and there were some glitches.	The presentation lacked planning and was unclear.	
Collaboration	All members participated regularly and responsibly.	Most team members participated regularly and responsibly.	Some team members participated regularly and responsibly.	The team did not work well together.	

Part 4:
RESOURCES

Print Materials

Armstrong, S., ed. 2002. *Edutopia: Success stories for learning in the digital age.* San Francisco: Jossey-Bass and the George Lucas Educational Foundation.

———. 2003. *Snapshots! Educational insights from the Thornburg Center.* Chicago: Starsong Publications.

Arter, J., and J. McTighe. 2001. *Scoring rubrics in the classroom: Using performance criteria for assessing and improving student performance.* Thousand Oaks: Corwin Press.

Bruce, B., ed. 2003. *Literacy in the information age: Inquiries into meaning making with new technologies.* Newark: International Reading Association, Inc..

Burmark, L. 2002. *Visual literacy: Learn to see, see to learn.* Alexandria: ASCD.

Cable in the classroom. 2002. *Thinking critically about media: Schools and families in partnership.* Alexandria.

Chen, M. 1994. *The smart parent's guide to kids' TV.* San Francisco: KQED Books.

Fang, I. 1997. *A history of mass communication: Six information revolutions.* Focal Press.

Gardner, H. 1983. *Frames of mind.* New York: Basic Books.

Hausman, C. 2000. *Lies we live by: Defeating double-talk and deception in advertising, politics, and the media*. Newark: Routledge.

i-Safe America. 2005–2006. *I-safe curriculum guide*. Carlsbad: i-Safe America.

Kilbourne, J. 1999. *Deadly persuasion: Why women and girls must fight the addictive power of advertising*. New York: The Free Press.

Littkey, D. 2004. *The big picture: Education is everyone's business*. Alexandria: ASCD.

Lockwood, S. 1997. *Media alert: 200 activities to create media-savvy kids*. Castle Rock: Hi Willow Research and Publishing.

Magid, L., and A. Collier. 2007. *MySpace unraveled: A parent's guide to teen social networking*. Berkeley: Peachpit Press.

McKenzie, J. 2007. *Leading questions: Managing complexity in the public and private sectors*. Seattle: FNO Press.

McTighe, J., and G. Wiggins. 1998. *Understanding by design*. Alexandria: ASCD.

My Hero Project, The. 2005. *My hero: Extraordinary people on the heroes who inspire them*. New York: Free Press.

O'Brien, P., ed. 2002. *Thinking critically about media: Schools and families in partnership*. Alexandria: Cable in the Classroom.

Porter, B. 2001. *Evaluating student computer-based products: Training and resource tools for using student scoring guides*. Sedalia: Bernajean Porter Consulting.

Prime Time Today. 2000. *Eye spy program: An interactive coloring book*. Littleton: Prime Time Today.

Richardson, W. 2006. *Blogs, wikis, podcasts, and other powerful web tools for classrooms*. Thousand Oaks: Corwin Press.

Schrock, K. 2001. *Writing and research on the computer*. Huntington Beach, CA: Teacher Created Materials.

Solomon, G., and L. Schrum. 2007. *Web 2.0: New tools, new schools*. Eugene: International Society for Technology in Education (ISTE).

Tapscott, D., and A. D. Williams. 2006. *Wikinomics: How mass collaboration changes everything*. New York: Portfolio.

Tate, M. A., and J. Alexander. 1999. *Web wisdom: How to evaluate and create information quality on the web*. Mahweh: Lawrence Erlbaum Associates, Inc..

Thornburg, D. 1992. *Brainstorms and lightning bolts: Thinking skills for the 21st century*. Chicago: Starsong Publications.

———. 1996. *Campfires in cyberspace*. Chicago: Starsong Publications.

———. 2006. *When the best is free: An educator's perspective on open source software*. Chicago: Starsong Publications.

Tyner, K. 1998. *Literacy in a digital world*. Mahweh: Lawrence Erlbaum Associates, Inc..

Warlick, D. 2002. *Raw materials of the mind: Teaching and learning in information and technology rich schools*. 3rd ed. Raleigh: The Landmark Project.

———. 2007. *Classroom blogging: A teacher's guide to blogs, wikis, and other tools that are shaping a new information landscape*. 2nd ed. Lulu.com.

Wurman, R. S. 2001. *Information anxiety 2*. Indianapolis: QUE.

Websites by Chapter

Chapter 1:

Metiri Group
http://www.metiri.com

Metiri Matrix: http://www.metiri.com/features.html

ISTE's NETS for Students
http://www.iste.org/Content/NavigationMenu/NETS/For_
Students/NETS_S.htm

About.com: Inventors: History of Communication
http://inventors.about.com/library/inventors/bl_history_of_
communication.htm

Wikipedia: History of Communication
http://en.wikipedia.org/wiki/History_of_communication

Nathan: Projects: A History of Communication 35,000 B.C. to A.D. 1998
http://www.nathan.com/projects/current/comtimeline.html

A World of Communication, ThinkQuest, 1999
http://library.thinkquest.org/26890/

Federal Communications Commission: History of Communication
http://www.fcc.gov/omd/history/

NASA History Division: Communications Satellites Short History
http://www.hq.nasa.gov/office/pao/History/satcomhistory.html

Chapter 2:

Polaroid Education Program
http://www.polaroid.com

The National Television Academy curriculum guide "'If It Bleeds, It Leads' and Other Lessons on Broadcast Journalism"
http://www.nationalstudent.tv/teachersmain.asp

http://www.nationalstudent.tv/information.asp

The Library of Congress
http://www.loc.gov

Checklist for an Informational Web Page
http://www3.widener.edu/Academics/Libraries/Wolfgram_
Memorial_Library/Evaluate_Web_Pages/Checklist_for_an_
Information_Web_Page/5720/

Original Web Evaluation Materials
http://www3.widener.edu/Academics/Libraries/Wolfgram_
Memorial_Library/Evaluate_Web_Pages/Original_Web_
Evaluation_Materials/6160/

The Onion
http://www.theonion.com/content/index

Chapter 3:

The Questioning Toolkit
http://questioning.org/Q7/toolkit.html

Grazing the Net: Raising a Generation of Free Range Students
http://www.fno.org/text/grazing.html

Jamie McKenzie's online journals
http://fno.org/JM/subscribe.html

The Buck Institute for Education
http://www.bie.org/index.php

Bloom's Taxonomy "Revised": Key Words, Model Questions & Instructional Strategies
http://www.ctap4.org/infolit/questions.htm

The Thornburg Center for Professional Development
http://www.tcpd.org

The Inquiry Page
http://inquiry.uiuc.edu

North Central Regional Educational Laboratory
http://www.ncrel.org/sdrs/areas/issues/students/learning/lr1kwlh.htm

Chapter 4:

Write Design Online—Graphic Organizers
http://www.writedesignonline.com/organizers/index.html

Institute of Food and Agricultural Sciences
http://edis.ifas.ufl.edu/UW003

Inspiration®
http://www.inspiration.com and http://www.inspiration.com/resources/index.cfm

Kidspiration®
http://www.kidspiration.com

Graphic Organizers: A Review of Scientifically Based Research
http://www.inspiration.com/resources/index.cfm?fuseaction=research

Cmap Tools
http://cmap.ihmc.us/

FreeMind
http://freemind.sourceforge.net/wiki/index.php/Main_Page

Wikka Wiki
http://wikkawiki.org/HomePage/

I Think … Therefore … MI! Multiple Intelligences in Education
http://surfaquarium.com/MI/

Howard Gardner, Multiple Intelligences and Education
http://www.infed.org/thinkers/gardner.htm

Concept to Classroom: Tapping into Multiple Intelligences
http://www.thirteen.org/edonline/concept2class/mi/index.html

The Graphic Organizer
http://www.graphic.org/links.html

NCREL
http://www.ncrel.org/sdrs/areas/issues/students/learning/lr1grorg.htm

Graphic Organizers Links
http://www.nvo.com/ecnewletter/graphicorganizers/

4 Blocks Literacy Framework: Graphic Organizers
http://www.k111.k12.il.us/lafayette/fourblocks/graphic_organizers.htm

ERIC Graphic Organizers: Elementary
http://www.indiana.edu/~reading/ieo/bibs/graphele.html

ERIC Graphic Organizers: Secondary Schools
http://www.indiana.edu/~reading/ieo/bibs/graphsec.html

Chapter 5:

Stanford University Libraries
http://fairuse.stanford.edu

Stanford University: Copyright Websites
http://fairuse.stanford.edu/web_resources/web_sites.html

The U.S. Copyright Office
http://www.copyright.gov

Copyright Office Basics: What Is Not Protected by Copyright
http://www.copyright.gov/circs/circ1.html#wnp

U.S. Copyright Office—Fair Use
http://www.copyright.gov/fls/fl102.html

Creative Commons
http://www.creativecommons.org

California Student Media Festival
http://www.mediafestival.org/

Hall Davidson
http://www.halldavidson.org

The Copyright Quiz
http://www.techlearning.com/techlearning/pdf/events/techforum/
tx05/2002TLQuiz.pdf

http://www.techlearning.com/db_area/archives/TL/2002/10/
copyright_quiz.php

The Copyright Quiz with answers
http://www.techlearning.com/db_area/archives/TL/2002/10/
copyright_answers.php

Two-Page Copyright Chart

http://halldavidson.org/downloads.html#anchor923173

Son of Citation Machine
http://citationmachine.net/?resize=1

MLA
http://www.mla.org/

Frequently Asked Questions about MLA Style
http://www.mla.org/publications/style/style_faq/

APA
http://www.apa.org

APA Style Guide
http://www.apastyle.apa.org/

Frequently Asked Questions about APA Style
http://www.apastyle.org/faqs.html

David Warlick's Landmark for School
http://www.landmark-project.com/index.php

Landmark Schools
http://www.landmark-project.com/permission.1.php.apa.org/

Chapter 6:

Four NETS
http://webquest.sdsu.edu/searching/fournets.htm

WebQuests
http://webquest.org.

Chapter 7:

Kathy Schrock's Guide for Educators
http://school.discoveryeducation.com/schrockguide/

The Learning Page
http://memory.loc.gov/learn

Checklist for an Information Web Pages
http://www3.widener.edu/Academics/Libraries/Wolfgram_
Memorial_Library/Evaluate_Web_Pages/Checklist_for_an_
Information_Web_Page/5720/

Feline Reactions to Bearded Men
http://www.improbable.com/airchives/classical/cat/cat.html

Dihydrogen Monoxide FAQ
http://www.dhmo.org/facts.html

Teacher Helpers: Critical Evaluation Information
http://school.discoveryeducation.com/schrockguide/eval.html

Nauset Public Schools Copyright and Fair Use Guidelines
http:\\nausetschools.org/fairuse.htm

Librarians' Internet Index
http://www.lii.org

Wall of Dreams
http://memory.loc.gov/learn/features/index.html#col_activities

Squeezing Documents: Close Reading of Primary Sources
http://memory.loc.gov/learn/educators/workshop/squeezing/baover.html

Students as Historians
http://memory.loc.gov/learn/educators/workshop/sah/hover.html

Prospecting in American Memory
http://memory.loc.gov/learn/educators/workshop/prospecting/prover.html

Searching American Memory
http://memory.loc.gov/learn/educators/workshop/search/index.html

Facilitators' Guide
http://memory.loc.gov/learn/educators/workshop/ssindex.html

Using Primary Sources in the Classroom—Lesson Suggestions
http://memory.loc.gov/learn/lessons/primary.html

Merriam-Webster Online
http://www.m-w.com

Free Dictionary
http://www.thefreedictionary.com

Dictionary.com
http://www.dictionary.reference.com

Spell It!
http://www.myspellit.com

Internet Public Library
http://www.ipl.org

Library of Congress: Kids, Families Section
http://www.loc.gov/families

Chapter 8:

SearchMobileComputing.com
http://searchmobilecomputing.techtarget.com/sDefinition/
0,,sid40_gci212057,00.html

CTAP Region 4 CyberSafety sites
http://www.ctap4.org/cybersafety/pi.htm
http://www.ctap4.org/cybersafety/cp.htm
http://www.ctap4.org/cybersafety/cb.htm

Greater Good Magazine
http://www.greatergoodmag.org

David Warlick's blog—"2¢ Worth: Teaching and Learning in the new education landscape"
http://davidwarlick.com/2cents/

Will Richardson's blog: "Weblogg-ed: Learning with the Read/Write Web"
http://weblogg-ed.com/about/

Anne Davis' EduBlog Insights
http://anne.teachesme.com/

Kathy Schrock's "Kaffeeklatsch"
http://kathyschrock.net/blog/

Kathy Schrock's Educational Technology Blog Listing
http://kathyschrock.net/edtechblogs.htm.

Blogs on Educational Blogging
http://supportblogging.com/Links+to+School+Bloggers

Blogger
http://www.blogger.com/start

Bloglines
http://www.bloglines.com

Edublogs
http://www.edublogs.com

Barbara Ganley's blogs
http://mt.middlebury.edu/middblogs/ganley/bgblogging/

Wikipedia
http://www.wikipedia.org

Wikispaces
http://www.wikispaces.com

Audacity
http://audacity.sourceforge.net

MySpace
http://www.myspace.com

Education Podcast Network
http://www.epnweb.org/

Facebook
http://www.facebook.com

Taking It Global
http://schoolibrary.org/res/library_2_0.htm

California School Library Association
http://www.takingitglobal.org

Chapter 9:

Learning with Technology Profile Tool
http://www.ncrtec.org/capacity/profile/profwww.htm

Project Approach
http://www.project-approach.com/definition.htm

Edutopia (The George Lucas Educational Foundation)
http:///www.edutopia.org

Project-Based Learning Teaching Module
http://www.edutopia.org/teaching-module-pbl

The Buck Institute for Education
http://www.bie.org/index.php/site/PBL/overview_pbl/

The Buck Institute's Project Based Learning Handbook
http://www.bie.org/index.php/site/PBL/pbl_handbook/

Problem Based Economics
http://www.bie.org/index.php/site/PBE/pbe_overview/

Problem Based Government
http://www.bie.org/index.php/site/PBG/pbg_overview/

The MY HERO Project
http://www.myhero.com

International Schools CyberFair 2008
http://www.globalschoolnet.org/gsncf//index.cfm

Island Movie
http://islandmovie.k12.hi.us/

California Student Media Project
http://www.mediafestival.org

National Student Television Awards
http://www.nationalstudent.tv/

ThinkQuest
http://www.thinkquest.org/library.html

International Schools CyberFair Rubric
http://www.globalschoolnet.org/gsncf/rubric//evalrubric.cfm

Rubistar
http://rubistar.4teachers.org/index.php

PBL Checklists
http://pblchecklist.4teachers.org/checklist.shtml

Rubric Machine

http://landmark-project.com/rubric_builder/index.php

Rubric Studio and Rubric Gallery

http://www.rcampus.com/rubricshellc.cfm?mode=gallery&sms=home&srcgoogle&gclid=CJy53ezf4JACFSosagodZBYjXQ

Specialized Search Engines and Directories

http://webquest.sdsu.edu/searching/specialized.html

There are approximately zillions of specialized search engines out there, as can be seen at Search Engine Guide (**http://www. searchengineguide.com/**). The list below is a selective subset of these search engines, chosen because they might help you find materials that will be useful as resources in a WebQuest. All of these links lead to sites that contain specific information that may not turn up when you do a general search of the Web using Altavista, Yahoo, or other search engines and directories. For a more comprehensive list, you might also want to check the Invisible-Website (**http://www.invisible-web.net**).

Directories Especially for Educators

Material appropriate for children	Yahoo! Kids KidsClick! ThinkQuest Entries Kids' Search Tool Ask for Kids	http://kids.yahoo.com http://www.kidsclick.org http://www.thinkquest.org/library http://www.rcls.org/ksearch.htm http://www.askforkids.com
School and university sites	SearchEdu.com	http://www.searchedu.com
Wired schools	Web66 School Registry Educational CyberPlayGround	http://web66.umn.edu http://www.edu-cyberpg.com/ Schools/default.asp
Multisubject starting points	BBC Schools BBC Learning Blue Web'n EduHound Education World Schrock's Guide Thinkfinity (formerly Marcopolo) SCORE Internet Scout FREE	http://www.bc.uk/schools http://www.bbc.co.uk/learning http://www.kn.pacbell.com/wired/ bluewebn http://www.eduhound.com http://www.education-world.com http://school.discovery.com/ schrockguide http://www.marcopolo-education.org. home.aspx http://www.score.k12.ca.us http://scout.wisc.edu http://www.free.ed.gov/sitemap.cfm

Children's software	California Learning Resource Network	http://www.clrn.org/home/
Lesson plans	ALI Units of Practice EdHelper Lesson Plans Page	http://ali.apple.com/ali/uops.shtml http://www.edhelper.com http://lessonplanspage.com
Curriculum standards	Education World	http://www.education-world.com/ standards/national/index.shtml
Info on educational issues	ERIC Search ERIC Facility	http://ericadr.piccard.csc.com/teams/ Login.do http://ericfacility.net/ericdigests/ index/

Search Engines and Databases Not Just for Educators

IF you're looking for ...	THEN check here:	OR type these in the location bar:
Encyclopedia entries	Encarta Wikipedia	http://encarta.msn.com http://en.wikipedia.org/wiki/Main_ Page
Magazine articles	Newslink Magazines	http://newslink.org/mag.html
Newspaper articles	Newslink Index	http://newslink.org
Current news	Google News	http://news.google.com
Blog postings	Technorati	http://www.technorati.com
Radio stations	radio-locator	http://www.radio-locator.com
Literature in the pubic domain	Google Book Search Online Books Search e-Books The Bartleby Library	http://www.books.google.com http://digital.library.upenn.edu/ books/ http://www.searchebooks.com http://www.bartleby.com
Copyrighted books in print	Amazon Barnes & Noble	http://www.amazon.com http://www.barnesandnoble.com

IF you're looking for ...	THEN check here:	OR type these in the location bar:
Images	Google Image Search Pics4Learning Fagan Finder eBay Postcards	http://www.google.com/advanced_image_search?hl=en http://pics.tech4learning.com http://www.faganfinder.com/img/ http://listings.ebay.com/aw/listings/list/category914/index.html
Images, sounds, videos of animals	JungleWalk	http://www.junglewalk.com
Live images from everywhere	EarthCam	http://www.earthcam.com
Primary-source documents	Library of Congress American Memory	http://lcwweb2.loc.gov/ammem/mdbquery.html
Federal (U.S.) legislation	THOMAS	http://thomas.loc.gov
Company information	Thomas Register Industrial Quick Search	http://www.thomasregister.com/ (free membership required) http://www.industrialquicksearch.com
Sounds	FindSounds.com	http://www.findsounds.com
Pictures and information about any product of the last two centuries	eBay	http://www.ebay.com
Biographies	Biographical Dictionary Biography.com Biography-Center Lives	http://www.s9.com/biography/ http://www.biography.com/search/ http://www.biography-center.com http://www.amillionlives.com
Maps	Perry-Casteñeda Maptech MapServer (topo)	http://www.lib.utexas.edu/maps/index.html http://mapserver.maptech.com
Country profiles	Atlapedia Online Kiosk: Journal of Geopolitics	http://www.atlapedia.com/online/country_index.html http://www.bay.k12.fl.us/pdk/kiosk/index.html

IF you're looking for …	THEN check here:	OR type these in the location bar:
State & county profiles	U.S. Census Dept. QuickFacts	http://quickfacts.census.gov/qfd/index.html
Medical information	HealthCentral.com	http://www.healthcentral.com/home/home.cfm
	OmniMedicalSearch	http://www.omnimedicalsearch.com
Military information	searchmil.com	http://www.searchmil.com
Trademarks	T.E.S.S.	http://www.uspto.gov/main/trademarks.htm
Patents	U.S. Patent and Trademark Office	http://www.uspto.gov/patft/index.html
TV episodes	Epguides	http://epguides.master.com/texis/master/search/mysite.html?
Movies, actors	Internet Movie Database	http://www.imdb.com
Measurement conversion	ConvertPlus	http://convertplus.com/en/
Shareware & freeware	Version Tracker C|Net Download Tucows	http://www.versiontracker.com http://www.download.com http://www.tucows.com
Even more search engines	Search-Engines2	http://www.search-engines-2.com

Last updated December 23, 2006.

The Copyright Quiz Answers

By Hall Davidson

Part I: Computers and Software

1. True. Technically, this should be done in the library. The law allows archival copies and, in some cases, lost, stolen, or damaged originals to be replaced with copies if the originals are unavailable or unreasonably priced.

2. False. As long as one copy is not being used simultaneously, it's okay to distribute the software via the server. However, when districts or schools fail to monitor and enforce simultaneous use, they get in trouble. (On a network, it's easy to track if a program is being used in more than one location.)

3. False. Alas, the teacher bought a product that isn't backward-compatible and should complain to the manufacturer. It's likely the law would deem it reasonable to install version 3.3 on the new machines (after removing version 4) until the issue is resolved.

4. False. Some interpretations of the 11th Amendment of the Constitution suggest that state schools may in fact be exempt from copyright prosecutions. However, following the guidelines encourages software and hardware makers to keep making quality products for us to buy.

5. False. Just as with a print encyclopedia, one student at a time has access to a piece of software. The number of students who can use a software program simultaneously is restricted to the number of copies the school purchased.

Part II: The Internet

6. True. The Web may be mined for resources. Download away (of course, don't hack into subscription sites)! But remember: You can't put these projects back up on the Web without permission from the copyright holders.

7. True. If the site really is protected, then this is considered okay. The school should monitor its Web hits, though, and make sure the outside world isn't sneaking in.

8. False. Educators may use "legitimately acquired" material without asking permission, but many file-sharing sites are suspect in this area. Use common sense to determine whether those peer-to-peer resources are legitimate or pirated. (You can also check copyright ownership at **www.copyright.gov** or **www.mpa.org**.)

9. True. MP3.com pays for its archives, so the material there is legitimately acquired. Be wary of some of the other peer-to-peer sites, however (see #8).

10. False. Legitimately acquired material can be used in classrooms. However, under the current law, no teacher can redistribute such material over the Net or any other medium. You can use it, but you can't spread it around.

Part III: Video

11. True. Video can be pulled into multimedia projects.

12. True. As authorized under the law, manufacturers are instituting blocking technology, so newer material like VHS rentals and DVDs block educators from their constitutional right to use material for teaching. It's time to begin complaining. In the meantime, educators should grab all the laser discs they can find. They're unblocked.

13. True. That's the other side of fair use. Just as you can use other people's intellectual property for educational purposes without permission, so can your own be used.

14. False. Video (like everything else) is not covered under fair use for entertainment or reward. The use described is entertainment, pure and simple. However, Disney will sell you a one-time license for $25 that makes this legal use. Call Disney at (818) 560-1000, ask for "rights," and prepare to trade faxes.

15. False. The current guidelines exclude the creation of video compilations. However, film clips for free are offered on FilmClipsOnline.com. (The VHS tape on American values is particularly good.) Email Michael Rhodes at imrhodes@msn.com or call (805) 984-5907.

Part IV: Multimedia

16. True.   Manufacturing these machines is now prohibited (it previously wasn't).   But teachers have the right to use material that is technologically blocked.   Personally, as a teacher, I would absolutely use it to unlock content for students, but I would absolutely not use it to make copies at home.

17. True. You may use the images in projects and post such images on the Web.   Some sites, like Disneyland and architectural landmarks, may be considered copyright material, however, and might ask you to remove the image. People (not selectively chosen) in public places are as a rule okay in photographs.

18. True.   See the Copyright and Fair Use Guidelines for Teachers chart (pages 230-231) for limitations on length.   To my mind, the music guidelines need to be rethought and broadened. Until then, look for CDs that are created royalty free.

19. False. This is not fair use. Yearbooks are not generally intended to be instructional. Plus, it's not permissible to use entire songs. If you're using pieces of songs and analyzing them as a reflection of the times students live in, that's different.

20. False. While fair use allows for the educational use of copyright material, it does so only if there is no anticipation of wider distribution.

Copyright and Fair Use Guidelines for Teachers

This chart was designed to inform teachers of what they may do under the law. Feel free to make copies for teachers in your school or district, or download a PDF version at

www.techlearning.com. More detailed information about fair use guidelines and copyright resources is available at www.halldavidson.net.

Medium	Specifics	What you can do	The Fine Print
Printed Material (short)	• Poem less than 250 words; 250-word excerpt of poem greater than 250 words • Articles, stories, or essays less than 2,500 words • Excerpt from a longer work (10 percent of work or 1,000 words, whichever is less) • One chart, picture, diagram, or cartoon per book or per periodical issue • Two pages (maximum) from an illustrated work less than 2,500 words, e.g., a children's book	• Teachers may make multiple copies for classroom use, and incorporate into multimedia for teaching classes. • Students may incorporate text into multimedia projects.	• Copies may be made only from legally acquired originals. • Only one copy allowed per student. • Teachers may make copies in nine instances per class per term. • Usage must be "at the instance and inspiration of a single teacher," i.e., not a directive from the district. • Don't create anthologies. • "Consumables," such as workbooks, may not be copied.
Printed Material (archives)	• An entire work • Portions of a work • A work in which the existing format has become obsolete, e.g., a document stored on a Wang computer	• A librarian may make up to three copies "solely for the purpose of replacement of a copy that is damaged, deteriorating, lost, or stolen."	• Copies must contain copyright information. • Archiving rights are designed to allow libraries to share with other libraries one-of-a-kind and out-of-print books.
Illustrations and Photographs	• Photograph • Illustration • Collections of photographs • Collections of illustrations	• Single works may be used in their entirety, but no more than five images by a single artist or photographer may be used. • From a collection, not more than 15 images or 10 percent (whichever is less) may be used.	• Although older illustrations may be in the public domain and don't need permission to be used, sometimes they're part of a copyright collection. Copyright ownership information is available at **www.loc.gov** or **www.mpa.org**.
Video (for viewing)	• Videotapes (purchased) • Videotapes (rented) • DVDs • Laserdiscs	• Teachers may use these materials in the classroom. • Copies may be made for archival purposes or to replace lost, damaged, or stolen copies.	• The material must be legitimately acquired. • Material must be used in a classroom or nonprofit environment "dedicated to face-to-face instruction." • Use should be instructional, not for entertainment or reward. • Copying OK only if replacements are unavailable at a fair price or in a viable format.

Category	Examples	Guidelines	
Video (for integration into multimedia or video projects)	• Videotapes • DVDs • Laserdiscs • Multimedia encyclopedias • QuickTime Movies • Video clips from the Internet	• Students "may use portions of lawfully acquired copyright works in their academic multimedia," defined as 10 percent or three minutes (whichever is less) of "motion media."	• The material must be legitimately acquired: a legal copy (not bootleg) or home recording. • Copyright works included in multimedia projects must give proper attribution to copyright holder.
Music (for integration into multimedia or video projects)	• Records • Cassette tapes • CDs • Audio clips on the Web	• Up to 10 percent of a copyright musical composition may be reproduced, performed, and displayed as part of a multimedia program produced by an educator or students.	• A maximum of 30 seconds per musical composition may be used. • Multimedia program must have an educational purpose.
Computer Software	• Software (purchased) • Software (licensed)	• Library may lend software to patrons. • Software may be installed on multiple machines, and distributed to users via a network. • Software may be installed at home and at school. • Libraries may make copies for archival use or to replace lost, damaged, or stolen copies if software is unavailable at a fair price or in a viable format.	• Only one machine at a time may use the program. • The number of simultaneous users must not exceed the number of licenses; and the number of machines being used must never exceed the number licensed. A network license may be required for multiple users. • Take aggressive action to monitor that copying is not taking place (unless for archival purposes).
Internet	• Internet connections • World Wide Web	• Images may be downloaded for student projects and teacher lessons. • Sound files and video may be downloaded for use in multimedia projects (see portion restrictions above).	• Resources from the Web may not be reposted onto the Internet without permission. However, links to legitimate resources can be posted. • Any resources you download must have been legitimately acquired by the Web site.
Television	• Broadcast (e.g., ABC, NBC, CBS, UPN, PBS, and local stations) • Cable (e.g., CNN, MTV, HBO) • Videotapes made of broadcast and cable TV programs	• Broadcasts or tapes made from broadcast may be used for instruction. • Cable channel programs may be used with permission. Many programs may be retained by teachers for years—see Cable in the Classroom (www.citonline.org) for details.	• Schools are allowed to retain broadcast tapes for a minimum of 10 school days. (Enlightened rights holders, such as PBS's *Reading Rainbow*, allow for much more.) • Cable programs are technically not covered by the same guidelines as broadcast television.

Sources: United States Copyright Office *Circular 21*: Sections 107, 108, and 110 of the Copyright Act (1976) and subsequent amendments, including the Digital Millennium Copyright Act; *Fair Use Guidelines for Educational Multimedia*; cable systems (and their associations); and *Copyright Policy and Guidelines for California's School Districts*, California Department of Education. Note: Representatives of the institutions and associations who helped to draw up many of the above guidelines wrote a letter to Congress dated March 19, 1976, stating "There may be instances in which copying that does not fall within the guidelines stated [above] may nonetheless be permitted under the criterion of fair use."

Acknowledgements

Many people contribute to a book, whether they know it or not. I'd like to thank all the thinkers who continue to work on ideas of literacy to make teaching and learning more effective and meaningful to students and teachers.

Many thanks to the contributors to this book who shared their work directly: Lynell Burmark, Hall Davidson, Bernie Dodge, Jamie McKenzie, and David Thornburg. Jan Alexander, Marsha Ann Tate, David Warlick, and the folks at Inspiration Software, Inc., generously gave permission to share website information and pages. Kathy Schrock, Gay Ducey, and Leni Donlan contributed thought-provoking interviews. And Bonnie Marks, Chip Bertram, Bernajean Porter, and David Thornburg shared their thoughts with me as well.

I hope this book is useful to you as you explore ideas of information literacy and help students expand their views on the topic.

> "Literacy is that which we actively construct. As we see new possibilities in the emerging media of the information age, we begin to change our literacy. In turn, as literacy practices of a community evolve, they shape the very media in which they are immersed. This coevolutionary process means that we can never freeze the activity of literacy and say that these are exactly the skills that need to be learned. Such a conclusion bodes ill for educational reform efforts based on monolithic definitions of literacy, predefined accountability criteria, or the linear accumulation of skills and knowledge" (Bertram Bruce, Literacy in the Information Age: Inquiries into Meaning Making with New Technologies, p. 337).

Sara Armstrong, Ph.D.
Berkeley, CA
saarmst@telis.org